T0201050

A PLUME BOOK

COLOR YOUR STYLE

DAVID ZYLA is the Emmy Award–winning costume designer and stylist for *All My Children*. He has been featured on *The View* and *CNN Style*, as well as in numerous magazines and newspapers, including the *New York Times* and the *Los Angeles Times*. He lives in New York City and Los Angeles.

color
your
style

HOW TO WEAR YOUR TRUE COLORS

DAVID ZYLA

Previously published as *The Color of Style*

A PLUME BOOK

PLUME
Published by the Penguin Group
Penguin Group (USA) Inc., 375 Hudson Street, New York, New York 10014, U.S.A. • Penguin
Group (Canada), 90 Eglinton Avenue East, Suite 700, Toronto, Ontario, Canada M4P 2Y3
(a division of Pearson Penguin Canada Inc.) • Penguin Books Ltd., 80 Strand, London WC2R
0RL, England • Penguin Ireland, 25 St. Stephen's Green, Dublin 2, Ireland (a division of Penguin
Books Ltd.) • Penguin Group (Australia), 250 Camberwell Road, Camberwell, Victoria 3124,
Australia (a division of Pearson Australia Group Pty. Ltd.) • Penguin Books India Pvt. Ltd.,
11 Community Centre, Panchsheel Park, New Delhi – 110 017, India • Penguin Group
(NZ), 67 Apollo Drive, Rosedale, North Shore 0632, New Zealand (a division of Pearson
New Zealand Ltd.) • Penguin Books (South Africa) (Pty.) Ltd., 24 Sturdee Avenue, Rosebank,
Johannesburg 2196, South Africa

Penguin Books Ltd., Registered Offices: 80 Strand, London WC2R 0RL, England

Published by Plume, a member of Penguin Group (USA) Inc. Previously published in a Dutton
edition as *The Color of Style*.

First Plume Printing, February 2011

The Library of Congress has catalogued the Dutton edition as follows:
Zyla, David.
    The color of style : a fashion expert helps you find colors that attract love, enhance your
power, restore your energy, make a lasting impression, and show the world who you really are /
by David Zyla.
      p. cm.
   ISBN 978-0-525-95153-7 (hc.)
   ISBN 978-0-452-29683-1 (pbk.)
   1. Beauty, Personal.   2. Clothing and dress.   3. Color in clothing.   4. Human skin color.
I. Title.
   RA778.Z953 2009
   646.7'2—dc22   2009026275

Printed in the United States of America
Set in Bembo
Original hardcover design by Spring Hoteling

ALL WOMEN DESERVE TO FEEL EMPOWERED AND LOOK FANTASTIC.
THIS BOOK IS DEDICATED TO THEM.

contents

color
your
style

introduction:

what color is your style?

my client Lizzie was in distress. She'd recently been promoted at the marketing firm she worked for, and her boss had told her that she was in line for a second promotion. After years of struggling along at the junior level, it seemed that Lizzie was finally about to break through.

But her boss had also told Lizzie that her personal style had raised some eyebrows and that she just "didn't make the right impression" for a top executive. Confused and a little hurt, Lizzie called me for a consultation.

As a stylist and a costume designer, I've worked for almost twenty years helping women express their own personal style, including politicians, models, TV actresses, and Broadway and film stars, such as Secretary of State Hillary Clinton, Cindy Crawford, Susan Lucci, Kelly Monaco, Christine Baranski, and Alfre Woodard, as well as scores of women who are celebrities only to the people who know them. One such woman was Lizzie's boss, who'd brought me to her Midwestern city to help her revamp her wardrobe. Thrilled with her own "style renaissance," she told Lizzie that I specialize in helping women discover their own unique *true colors:* the colors that define their *authentic style.*

Authentic Style:

An integral, personal style that allows you to attract love, claim your power, balance your energy, and reveal who you truly are by choosing the colors, clothes, and objects that express your authentic self.

But while her boss had been eager, Lizzie was reluctant. "I hate the idea of just buying some boring old suits and I wouldn't really know how to pick them out anyway," Lizzie told me, nervously drumming her fingers on the kitchen table. "I'm going through so much right now—I can't believe clothes are what I have to think about."

As we talked, I could see that Lizzie was indeed going through a lot. Besides the new challenges at work, her husband had recently lost his job, leading to serious friction in their marriage. One of her children was struggling with a drug problem; another had a learning disability and was having trouble in school.

Yet despite all her worries about the daunting challenges she faced, I could see a real strength in Lizzie, a bedrock of determination and courage. Despite her frustrated, edgy voice, I could sense a naturally joyous person, the kind of woman who walks into a room and suddenly makes everyone feel that not only is she fabulous—they are, too. I could see why her boss thought so highly of Lizzie, enough to go out of her way to recommend me.

As I went through Lizzie's wardrobe, I could also see why eyebrows had been raised. Here she was about to turn forty, yet she dressed like the teenager she had been twenty years ago—literally. Her entire look was from the 1980s: big hair, streaked with color; bold makeup, with bright blush on her prominent cheekbones; large, painted nails. When I met her, she was dressed in a short black skirt, a sizzling blue tank top, and an acid-pink-and-blue-patterned blazer with enormous shoulder pads—all colors and patterns that did not connect. And when she showed me her closet, I could see more of those eighties "power" thunderbolt designs and electric hues: teal, bright white, royal purple.

It wasn't a question of age or fashion. Lizzie's colors would have looked terrific on someone with different skin tones, eyes, and hair. In fact, I'd recently had a consultation with a fifty-year-old client in Memphis to whom I'd recommended just this palette. But for Lizzie, these colors were all wrong because they failed to express her true self.

I looked at Lizzie's green-flecked hazel eyes, her deep brown hair, and her glowing beige skin, and thought immediately, *Bronze Autumn*. When I work with a client, I first identify her **true colors:** the five major hues of her palette: **essence, romantic, dramatic, energy,** and **tranquil,** plus her three neutrals, **First Base** (her version of black), **Second Base** (her version of brown), and **Third Base** (her version of khaki).

Once I know a client's **true colors,** I'm able to tell which **Season** she is: Spring, Summer, Autumn, or Winter. Each *Season* corresponds to her basic coloring—hair, eyes, skin—and also to some aspects of her personality.

But four categories are hardly enough to express all the marvelous variety that each of us brings into the world. So within each **Season** are six **Archetypes:** distinct types combining the coloring, personality, and overall style that can help you hone in on the perfect colors, clothes, and objects that you need to express your authentic self. Your **true colors,** your **Season,** and your **Archetype** are the basic ingredients of your own **authentic style.**

Creating Your *Authentic Style*

- Identify your **true colors:** your **essence, romantic, dramatic, energy,** and **tranquil** colors, plus your **three bases**—neutrals that are your own individualized versions of black, brown, and khaki.
- Discover your **Season:** Spring, Summer, Autumn, or Winter.
- Claim your **Archetype:** one of six distinct types to be found in each season, which will give you further ideas for colors, clothes, and objects that express your authentic self.

As a Bronze Autumn, Lizzie fit an **Archetype** that I think of as the Divine Diva. She was made to draw attention—to walk into a room and have all eyes turn to her—but it wasn't going to happen unless she chose the colors, clothes, and objects that revealed who she truly was.

"You know," Lizzie was saying, "it's been a really tough few months. Between my job and everything at home . . ." Her voice trailed off. "I just don't feel like I've got it in me to take on one more thing. I mean, *clothes*? Really?"

"I can see you're going through a lot," I said with sympathy. "And given everything you're dealing with, I can see how clothes might not seem so important. What I'd like to suggest, though, is that it would actually help you to solve your problems if you'd change some of the things in your closet."

Lizzie stared at me, unable to believe I was serious.

"It's true," I told her. "If you know your colors, then you know yourself. And if you dress like the person you really are—the person I can see in your hair and eyes and skin—you start tapping into your own unique energy and freeing resources you didn't even know you had. Finding your true colors is one way to get in touch with your true self—and what could be more powerful than that?"

Your *True Colors*

Essence Color: The color that harmonizes your skin tones and reveals your most genuine, open, and essential self; your version of white; wear it when you are having an intimate conversation, when you are meditating, or when you want to be completely open and honest.

Romantic Color: The color taken from your flushed skin, which reveals your passion, your sexual energy, and your romantic self; your version of red; wear it on a hot date, a romantic evening, or any time you want your passion to show.

Dramatic Color: The color taken from the shade of your veins, which reveals your power, your charisma, and your sense of authority; your version of blue; wear it on a job interview, for a formal presentation, or any time you want to make a strong impression.

Energy Color: The color seen in the darkest part of your iris (not the ring around your iris), which taps into the deepest sources of your energy; helps you restore and balance your energy; wear it when you want to be calm, self-possessed, and centered, such as at a family reunion, a meeting with your child's teacher, or a corporate retreat.

Tranquil Color: The color found in the lightest part of your iris, which taps into the deepest sources of your tranquility; helps you relax and release stress; wear it when you want to recover from a challenging situation, such as after a long day at work.

Lizzie was understandably skeptical. But she allowed me to take her through the process of identifying her *true colors:* her *essence* color, a flattering dark beige that almost seemed to be a direct extension of her own skin; her *romantic* color, a vivid orange-red taken from the color of her flushed skin; and her *dramatic* color, a striking jade green that came from the deepest tone of her veins. By the time we chose her *energy* and *tranquil* colors—a bright parrot green and a pale olive, taken from the darkest and the lightest parts of her iris—Lizzie was overcome.

"I've always loved these colors," she told me. "But I never thought I could wear them."

"Look," I told her, "your coloring tells me a lot about you. You're very strong and earthy and warm and caring. And when you wear these colors, you're going to be telling other people who you are, too."

Lizzie looked at the *true colors* we had identified for her, which also included her *three bases:* individual versions of neutral colors that correspond to black (most formal), brown (warmer and less formal), and khaki (playful and informal). For some people, the *three bases* really are black, brown, and khaki. When you understand the colors of *your* style, though, you come to see that even neutral colors are highly personal. For many people, "black" is better expressed as midnight blue, aubergine, or charcoal gray; "brown" might be gold, mushroom gray, or camouflage green; and "khaki" could be a deep rose beige, a subtle silver, or a lavender-hued taupe.

Your *True Colors*

First Base: The color found in the ring around your iris; your most formal and powerful neutral; your version of black.

Second Base: The color taken from the darkest shade of your hair; a warmer and less formal neutral; your version of brown.

Third Base: The color seen in the lightest version of your hair; a playful and informal neutral; your version of khaki.

NOTE: Whether your hair is natural or dyed, these colors are easiest to see on the underside.

For Lizzie, "black" was a deep chocolate, just as "brown" was a warm rust and "khaki" an oyster white. As soon as I held some fabric swatches next to her face, she could see how flattering these new colors would be. True black made Lizzie's features look harsh and gaunt, while *her* "black"—deep chocolate— made her eyes glow. Likewise, a true medium brown made Lizzie's face and hair look dull, while *her* "brown"—warm rust—instantly gave her more color. True khaki did nothing for Lizzie, but *her* "khaki"—oyster white—made her look relaxed and ready to play.

I could see Lizzie's mood change as each color came to join her. Of course, she enjoyed seeing how flattering these new shades were, and she clearly got a lot of pleasure from realizing how attractive she could be. But Lizzie wasn't only responding to the ego boost. She was also feeling a kind of deep recognition, the thrill of seeing an image in the mirror that revealed aspects of herself that had been hidden until now.

"I've never worn any of these colors," she said finally. "But

I see what you mean. You're describing me, and they're describing me. I don't know how—but they are."

The Joys of Finding Your *Authentic Style:* What My Clients Have Told Me

"It seems to be easier to make friends."

"I'm dating more often."

"I find it easier to ask for what I want at work."

"I'm getting more professional recognition."

"I'm thinking differently about what I want in life—and taking some new steps to get it."

"I'm less anxious about fitting in and more willing to be myself."

"I'm less shy about asking someone out on a date!"

"It used to bother me when people noticed me—but now I actually like it!"

"Friends and colleagues have told me they want to attend a party just to see what I'll be wearing! I feel like the permanent guest of honor."

"I have more energy—and I'm also more relaxed. It's like I've finally found the right balance."

Lizzie was experiencing the joy of finding her *authentic style:* an integral and personal style that allows you to attract love, claim your power, balance your energy, and reveal who you truly are by choosing the colors, clothes, and objects that express your authentic self. Finding your *true colors* and your *authentic style*—that is, choosing the colors and elements that support and reveal who you really are—enables you to show your true self to the world. When you're in tune with the colors, clothes, and objects you have chosen, you allow others to recognize you, you become more attractive, and you tend to feel more energized, confident, and clear.

I've seen dozens of women like Lizzie blossom as they begin to wear the colors that are right for them. All of a sudden, they're getting the promotions they deserve or the dates they've desired, reconnecting to their families in new ways, rediscovering hidden ambitions or lost creativity. They didn't have to lose ten pounds or start wearing a ton of makeup or spend a fortune buying haute couture. They only had to choose the colors, clothes, and objects that expressed their authentic selves.

The Elements of Your *Authentic Style*

True Colors: The colors that express your authentic self

Season: The set of colors and personality traits corresponding to one of the four seasons of the year; essential for understanding the colors, clothes, and objects that express your authentic self

Archetype: The set of colors, style choices, and personality traits corresponding to one of the six subtypes of a *Season*; essential for understanding the colors, clothes, and objects that express your authentic self

---

Once you master the principles of your **authentic style,** you'll never be a slave to fashion. Instead, you'll be empowered to create your own fashion, based on your **true colors,** your **Season,** and your **Archetype.** You'll develop an unerring sense of the colors, clothes, and objects that belong in your life: on your body, in your home, and surrounding you at work. You'll save time both when you dress and when you shop, because you'll never have to wonder which garments to choose or which colors to wear—you'll *know* exactly what's right for you. And finally, when you go shopping, instead of relying upon the hope of inspiration jumping off a hanger, you'll be able to make a beeline for just those clothes that express your authentic self.

You'll save money, too, because once you know your *authentic style,* you'll never buy something that is wrong for you—no more shopping mistakes! Plus you'll know lots of creative ways to make a single garment do double and triple duty, making it look new each time. Because you know how to vary and combine color in creative ways—putting a *First Base* suit together with an *essence* blouse or a *dramatic* shell, for example—you can purchase far fewer garments and still always have something fabulous to wear. Even if there are only a few key items in your closet, the way you combine and accessorize them will create the impression of an extensive wardrobe.

More important, when you're dressing in your *authentic style,* everything you wear will express and support your best self, the most authentic—and therefore the most attractive—version of who you are. Surrounding yourself with the colors, clothes, and objects that express your authentic self can genuinely transform your sense of yourself and your world. Revealing your true self rather than a false one is the best way I know to attract the good things you deserve and create the life you truly want.

After helping so many women find their *authentic style,* I've come to believe that when we bring our true inner selves out into the world, making ourselves visible through our colors, clothes, and objects, we empower ourselves. We are also open to new possibilities for connecting with others, whether networking at the office, finding a new romance, or deepening the relationships we already have.

It makes sense to me that my clients find more responsive friends, lovers, and colleagues as they embody their **true colors** and their **authentic style,** because they're sharing in visual form exactly who they are. The riches of friendship, love, and happiness are there, because they are adorning themselves in the garments and accessories that reveal their authentic personality and spirit. What an extremely powerful place from which to operate: being noticed as the unique individual that is you!

Certainly Lizzie discovered the power of her **authentic style** when she started dressing in the rich chocolate browns and dazzling greens that brought out her Bronze Autumn nature. Before I received an excited call from Lizzie (she got her promotion), I had heard from her boss, who sounded almost bewildered as she thanked me for the wonderful enhancement.

"She's like a different person," Lizzie's boss told me. "I don't even know how to describe it. She hasn't gone into a lot of detail with me, but I know she's made some changes on the home front, with her husband and her kids. I think things have gotten a lot better there, too."

Lizzie's boss paused, searching for words. "She looks terrific, of course, but it's more than that. She looks strong. Successful. Confident." Suddenly she laughed in discovery. "You know what it is?" she said. "Lizzie finally looks like herself."

PART I:

showing your true colors

I

it's all in the palm of your hand:

learning how to see

even though I work with color, style, and clothing every day, the power of color never ceases to amaze me. When we wear the colors that reveal our true self, we flourish. When we wear colors that conceal that authentic self, we flounder—even when we have the looks, talent, and personality to succeed.

One of my most dramatic encounters with the power of color came, appropriately enough, at the callbacks for a new musical that I'd been called in to design. Costume designers don't usually attend callbacks (the second phase of auditions, when the top candidates are "called back" for a final decision). But since the show was going to be rehearsing out of town, this seemed like the most efficient way for me to get a good look at the actors I'd be dressing.

Two women had been called in for a final shot at the leading role. The first actress walked through the door wearing a simple dress of peachy pink. The outfit was a bit out of style, not quite the latest fashion, but it really flattered her. In fact, when she burst through the door, we saw a blur of vital color who struck us all as a force to be reckoned with. She strode over to the piano, gave the accompanist her music, and broke into song. Her voice was lovely—not the best I'd ever heard, but certainly quite good. Her leading man came in, and when they read together, I saw that she was a fine actress—again, not the best I'd ever seen, but a strong, effective presence.

When the door opened a second time and her rival walked in, the contrast couldn't have been sharper. This second woman also wore a simple dress, but in a too-bright shade of red that was far too vivid and intense for her delicate coloring. Clearly someone had told her that "red" equals "sexy," but this actress was a Buoyant Spring, an *Archetype* whose ideal shade of "red"—her *romantic* color—was a crisp, glowing melon. The fire engine red she wore would have looked terrific on another *Archetype,* such as a Vital Winter, but on this actress, it looked as though she was trying too hard.

This second actress sang her song, and in my opinion, her voice was clearly much better than the first actress's, as were her delivery, phrasing, and emotional power. She played the spoken scene with the leading man, and again, I thought, her work was far superior to the first woman's. Even her face, I realized, was more classically beautiful—once I managed to see past the obstacle of that fire engine red. On every count, it seemed, she would have been the better choice.

But when the door closed behind her, the director turned to the casting director and they said, practically in unison, "Well, it's pretty obvious who we're going with." Even though the second actress had a prettier face, was more talented, and was blessed with a better voice, the first actress seemed to both men to be the clear winner—merely because she had dressed in her *authentic style.*

As someone who works with clothes and color all the time, I had found a way to see past the second actress's "disguise"— the color that hid who she truly was. These other men weren't willing or able to go beyond their first impressions. When they looked at the first actress, she appeared so at home in that peach-colored dress that her talent, beauty, and spirit simply shone. When they looked at the second actress, they didn't even know what they were missing. That unfortunate red might as well have been a burlap bag, hiding her talent, her personality, and even her beauty.

For a moment, perhaps, the second actress had held that part in the palm of her hand. But then, at odds with the colors she had chosen, unable to show herself as she truly was, she let her chances go.

CLAIMING YOUR PERSONAL BEAUTY

In one of those coincidences that seem to happen so often in the entertainment world, I ended up, some months later, with that second actress as a client. I'm happy to report that once she learned her true colors and her authentic style, her natural beauty and talent burst forth, and she hasn't stopped working since. But her story has stuck with me over the years, partly because she was so exceptionally beautiful. So often, when I've spoken with new clients, they've said dismissively, "Oh, so-and-so is such a pretty girl—she can wear anything! It's going to be a lot harder to make me look good."

In fact, neither part of that is true. My actress client *was* an unusually lovely woman—but when she wasn't wearing her ***true colors,*** her beauty couldn't shine. And many women who are not classically beautiful can nonetheless command a room with their sexual appeal, their charisma, or their confidence. Think of women such as Barbra Streisand, Queen Latifah, and Whoopi Goldberg.

Not a classic beauty in the bunch—but each of those women have the power to turn heads, and not just because she is famous. In fact, most of them became famous *because* of their star quality. Their beauty comes not from meeting some external set of standards but rather because they look like themselves.

Something extra gets released when a person really understands herself, and when she chooses colors, clothes, and objects that reveal who she really is. A woman in her **true colors** looks whole, not fragmented; like her full self rather than some dim shadow. Women who reveal their full selves hold their power and their beauty in the palm of their hand—and they make the most of it. You can, too.

TRAINING YOUR EYE

So now it's time to begin choosing the colors that are going to bring out your true self. In the following three chapters, you'll learn how to find your true colors, identifying your essence, romantic, dramatic, energy, and tranquil colors as well as your three bases. In later chapters, you'll go on to discover your Season and claim your Archetype, which will help you identify even more facets of your authentic style. You'll also learn how each color affects your emotions and the emotions of those around you, so that you can use color to create the moods and impressions appropriate to each occasion.

Creating Your *Authentic Style*

- Identify your *essence, romantic, dramatic, energy,* and *tranquil* colors, plus your *three bases*—neutrals that are your own individualized versions of black, brown, and khaki.
- Discover your *Season:* Spring, Summer, Autumn, or Winter.

- Claim your *Archetype:* one of six distinct types to be found in each season, which will give you further ideas for colors, clothes, and objects that express your authentic self.

First, though, I'd like to help you train your eye to identify all the subtle nuances of shade, tint, and hue. So let's go shopping. No, not in a department store or boutique—not yet, anyway! I want to send you on a field trip to your local grocery store.

Now, don't panic. I'm not going to suggest some reality show exercise where you have to create haute couture out of celery stalks and coffee filters. I am going to send you over to the produce section, where you can focus strictly on color and not be overwhelmed by hemlines, designer labels, and price tags. Of course, the colors in a grocery store are nothing new to you—but neither is your image in the mirror. So let's find out just how closely you can look at a familiar sight—and how many new aspects of color you can perceive.

Ways to Talk About Color

Research has shown that humans have the ability to differentiate up to ten million subtleties between colors. Are you really "seeing" the colors that you choose to wear? Here are some ways to talk about color that might help you notice more of those subtle differences:

- *Saturation:* How bright is it? A bright, intense color is highly saturated; a pale, delicate color is less saturated.
- *Value:* How light or dark is it? Think about a bar of deep, dark chocolate and a cup of cocoa into which some whipped cream has already melted. Both colors are versions of "chocolate brown" but the two colors have different values—and might well look flattering on different people.

- *Tint:* A color that has been "mixed" with white, making it lighter. Pink, for example, is a tint of red. Being sensitive to tint is important because a color that might not work on you in one tint could potentially be fantastic if it was a little bit lighter or a little bit darker.

- *Shade:* A color that has been "mixed" with black, making it dark. Navy, for example, is a shade of blue. Again, a color that might not work on you in one shade could be the perfect choice in a slightly different shade.

- *Tone:* A color that has been "mixed" with another color. Think, for example, of the differences between yellow-green, "pure" green, blue-green, and brownish green. You might call any of these tones "green"—but some might look terrific on you, while others might make your skin look sallow, flushed, or blotchy.

- *Temperature:* Is the color in question "warm" or "cool"? Warm colors evoke the sunlight and tend to include red, orange, yellow, and brown. Cool colors evoke the moonlight and tend to include blue, green, and purple. However, within these basic groupings, we can notice even more subtleties. Think, for example, of the deep blue-red of a Concord grape. That's a much cooler red than, say, the warm orange-red of a tomato. By the same token, the yellowish green of a lime is much warmer than the deep emerald green of spinach. Even noncolors, like white, black, and gray, can become cooler or warmer if they are mixed with subtle tones of pink, yellow, green, or lavender.

Got it? Now you can start thinking about color in more specific ways: "Oops, that color isn't quite saturated enough for me"; "I have to be careful—if this color goes a shade darker, it doesn't work for my skin"; or "There's a little too much yellow in that green—I need a cooler tone."

Okay, let's start with red. Sounds simple, right? There are lots of reds in the produce section: apples, beets, radishes, peppers, strawberries, tomatoes, maybe even cherries and plums if they're in season. Start by noticing and naming to yourself as many different colors, shades, tints, and tones as you can. Here are some reds that we'll revisit in the next chapter when we identify your **romantic** color. How many of them can you discover at the grocery store?

True reds:	clear red, fire engine red, Christmas red, crimson, scarlet, ruby, blue red, vermilion
Pinkish reds:	geranium, watermelon, strawberry
Purple reds:	bright cherry, dark cherry, cranberry, raspberry, maroon, mulberry, magenta, grappa
Orange reds:	Chinese red, cayenne, terra-cotta, paprika, brick red, orange red, tomato, tangerine, flame
Brownish reds:	rusty burgundy, claret, cinnamon, Indian red brown, port, cool brick, rusty brick

Is your head spinning? Rest your eyes for a few moments by looking at another color—maybe the range of greens available among the cucumbers, green peppers, basil, coriander, and romaine—and then turn your gaze to the humble tomato. Select a few different kinds—regular, plum, and cherry—and line them up somewhere you can look at them for a few minutes, maybe in the top section of your shopping cart. Set the alarm on your watch or phone and examine the tomatoes for at least three minutes; five if you can muster up the patience.

Now, how many different shades, tints, values, and degrees of saturation can you find? Can you find hints of blue-red, yellowish tones, and orange as well as red? Can you identify scarlet, crimson, terra-cotta, brick? Take a moment to find a strawberry, a raspberry, and an open watermelon and compare: How do those reds differ from those of the tomato you're looking at? (This is a technique that you may need to use when you finally do get to your local store and you've found a gorgeous red dress that might not be *your* red.)

If you're enjoying your tour of colors, you can take it up a notch, comparing the different yellows among lemons and grapefruits, for example, or the different shades of orange among oranges, apricots, peaches, and tangerines. Or, if your patience is wearing thin, take a quick look at some of the other colors: the distinctive blue of blueberries, the aubergine purple of eggplants, the many, many different shades of green. The more colors you can notice and name, the sharper your eye will be when it's time to find your true colors in your skin, your eyes, and your hair.

Sight and Insight: Opening Your Vision

Most of us have trouble being objective about ourselves, especially when it comes to our true colors. If I asked you what color your hair is, for example, you'd probably answer "brown," "blond," "red," "black," or "gray." Okay, but if I asked you to find six different tones in your hair, could you name them without looking in a mirror? I'm sure you could tell me whether your eyes are brown, blue, green, or gray. But could you identify, without looking, the lightest and darkest tones of your iris and the shade of the ring around the iris's rim? If you're like most people, you may not even be able to name the shade of your flushed skin or identify the exact shade of blue, green, or purple in your veins.

Well, now's the time to change all that. In the next several chapters, we're going to identify key colors in your skin, eyes, and hair, and then we're going to see how color expresses different aspects of personality and evokes different emotions in yourself and in others. That is the heart of *The Color of Style*. But before we start exploring the links between color and emotion, I'd like you to practice looking at yourself objectively—without emotion—so that you can expand your vision and see your colors truly. You may be surprised at what you find!

Let Go of Your Color Bias

We all have color biases—how could we help it? "Black is slimming." "Red is sexy." "Pale blue is for old ladies." "Orange is tacky." As a High Autumn whose *romantic*-color version of "red" is a warm, bright shade of tangerine, I've struggled with color biases myself. For many years I associated tangerine with a particularly awful shirt that I received as a tenth birthday present. I never wore that shirt, but because I loved the aunt who gave it to me, it hung in my closet for years, a constant reminder of how much I hated orange.

Then I realized that my problem wasn't with the color. What I found unappealing was the shirt's itchy polyester knit, its scoop neckline, and its heavily embroidered scene of the Rocky Mountains, splashed right across the chest. That shirt didn't reflect my personality at all—but the color did.

Luckily I learned to overcome my color bias and to accept that tangerine is the color that best expresses my vitality, my passion, and my sense of romance. As a result I have enjoyed many warm, friendly evenings—and my fair share of dates!—in my orange sweaters, shirts, and ties.

Many people have asked me over the years whether there are any colors that are just plain "ugly" and don't look good on anyone. My answer is a firm no. Every color is beautiful in its correct context.

So, as you embark on your color journey, please keep your mind—and your eyes—open. When I identify *true colors* for my clients, most people have already sampled about half of the colors I suggest for them. The other half, though, often come as a complete surprise. Even if you have incredible color instincts, you, too, may discover one or two or six new hues that you never realized you could wear—hues that bring out whole new aspects of your true self. Pretend that you've lived your life in a black-and-white film and that you've just now emerged from the screen. Wow! Color! You would feel as though a sixth sense had suddenly been added to your repertoire, every color fresh and new, with no connotations whatsoever. That's the kind of open mind—and open eyes—that we're going for.

Eight Steps to Seeing Your *True Colors*

1. *Find a quiet room with soft, natural light.* Ideally you'll pick a space that is uncluttered and mellow. I find it helps to put a piece of white paper under your hand so that you aren't influenced by the mahogany wood stain of the table or the cobalt blue of the sink tile. If you have long hair, pull it out of your face so you can focus on other colors for a while.

2. *Take a good look at your hand.* Take a deep breath, relax your face and eyes, and then focus on your hand. Yes, that's right. Everything you want—love,

power, and the key to your own true self—is all in the palm of your hand!

At first, your hand may seem familiar to you—extremely so. But, like the produce at the grocery store, it's probably so familiar that you no longer really see it. Allow yourself to notice details that you usually look right past: the lines, nooks, and crannies that swirl across your palm; the way each of your fingers has its own unique shape and angle.

3. **Start to notice color.** You may be used to thinking of your hand as a single, simple color, but when you look at it more closely, what do you see? Can you distinguish, for example, between the color of the mound below your thumb and the shade of your middle finger's center joint? Can you see how your skin is more flushed at the tip of your thumb, and at the bottom of your palm below your little finger? What about the middle of your hand? Can you see yet another color? Take a few moments simply to relax, observe, and notice.

4. **Identify different colors.** Now that you've become aware of different colors, try to name them. Do you see beige, peach, olive, salmon, honey, pecan, coffee? How about cream, rose-beige, mahogany, or chestnut? Try to identify at least five different colors, from the center of your palm to the central joints of your fingers and everything in between. Notice, too, what types of colors there are—warm like the glow of a candle flame or cool like moonlight? Is the overall tone white, pinkish, yellow, golden, beige, or brown? As you did in the grocery store, notice the shaded areas, the saturated areas, and all the different tones,

jotting down every color you notice. As always, be
as precise as possible. Here are some color words to
get you started:

- **Whites:** milky white, porcelain, creamy ivory,
  bisque, parchment, pearl
- **Pinks:** cream with an undertone of peach or rose;
  cameo, seashell, cool pink, ice pink, dusty rose,
  violet rose, peach, peach pink
- **Yellows:** yellow brown, yellow beige, sand
- **Golds:** honey, golden beige, golden brown, olive
  gold
- **Beiges:** pale beige, rose beige, greige (grayish
  beige), copper beige, tawny beige, brown beige
- **Browns:** olive, rose brown, gray brown, mahogany, chestnut, toasted golden brown, cedar, caramel, bronze, ash, blue black

Look, too, at the flushed portion of your hand—
the tips of your fingers and, often, your lower
palm. Which of these colors can you see?

- **Pinks:** ballet pink, cool shell pink, shocking pink,
  rose pink, Barbie doll pink, carnation, coral pink,
  bright coral, cool dusty pink, salmon, dusty rose,
  fuchsia, dusty fuchsia, tulip
- **Oranges:** peach, peach coral, burnt peach, light
  orange, Creamsicle, apricot, deep apricot, rusty
  brick, orange red, tomato
- **Reds:** clear red, bright cherry, dark cherry, poppy,
  fire engine red, Christmas red, Chinese red, ruby,
  blue red, crimson, scarlet, vermilion, rusty burgundy, brick red, strawberry, mulberry, raspberry,
  claret, geranium, watermelon
- **Purples:** cranberry, maroon, magenta, burgundy

- **Browns:** cayenne, terra-cotta, paprika, cinnamon, flame, tangerine, Indian red brown, cool brick, rust

5. ***Now focus on your veins.*** In natural light, look at the inner side of your wrist. Can you pick up different shades of blue, purple, and green?

   - **Blues:** ultramarine, cerulean, cornflower blue, pacific blue, electric blue, blueberry, bluebell, deep sky blue, Wedgwood, Danube blue, deep sapphire, blue violet, deep teal, peacock blue, turquoise blue, lapis blue, Egyptian blue, Nile blue, Venetian blue, deep blue green, clear sapphire, cobalt blue, royal blue, Persian indigo

   - **Purples:** royal purple, eggplant, black plum, periwinkle dust, periwinkle, pansy, wisteria lilac, clear violet, powdered periwinkle, hyacinth, lavender, blackberry, amethyst, plum, violet

   - **Blue Greens:** aquamarine, aqua, clear turquoise, robin's egg blue

   - **Greens:** Kelly green, sea green, shamrock, vivid jade, frosted wintergreen, English holly, clear emerald, evergreen, spruce, cool spruce, robin's egg green, ocean green, cool jade, emerald, wintergreen, green pea, juniper, Viridian green, racing green, pine, Persian green, jade, turquoise green, peacock green, deep fern, cypress, seaweed green, evergreen, dark emerald

6. ***Look at your eyes.*** Once you've picked up on how many shades and tints are in your hand, extend your new supervision to your eyes. If possible, study your eyes in a magnifying mirror under natural light. Notice the flecks and depths of colors in your irises,

and the different shades of black, dark brown, and purple in your pupils. Have you always taken your eyes as "just blue" and never noticed the sage green flecks in them? Did you ever see the parrot green cast to your "brown" eyes? Or the tiny notes of slate blue and gold? Is the brown of your eye warm or cool? Perhaps your eyes are one temperature—say, a warm brown—while your flecks are cool—blue gray or deep green. Or perhaps you've always thought of your eyes as "chocolate brown," while closer to your pupil you can find a lighter, "chocolate milk" tint. Jot down whatever eye colors you find, using this list to get you started:

- **Blues:** true blue, powder blue, clear blue, ice blue, lapis blue, aqua, turquoise, teal blue, steel blue
- **Purples:** indigo, blue violet, violet
- **Grays:** blue gray, pale gray, deep gray
- **Greens:** clear green, ice green, cool green, leaf green, olive, green gray, gray green, silver green, green with golden flecks, parrot, golden olive, verde, hazel
- **Golds:** amber, topaz, green gold, brown gold, brown with golden flecks
- **Browns:** light brown, rose brown, golden brown, deep warm brown, deep brown, black brown, off black

7. *Focus on your hair.* Now it's time to move beyond "blond," "brunette," and "redhead" to a more specific look at those lovely locks. If you're a blonde, can you find some deep green-gold undertones? As a brunette, can you discover an aubergine cast beneath the brown, or perhaps a bluish note on top

of the black? If you color your hair, you may have trouble finding as many subtle shades and variations as you could in natural hair, but give it a try. And whether your hair is natural or dyed, use the underside: That's where the color becomes easiest to see. Expect the unexpected—and then write down three shades, from lightest to medium to darkest. Here's a list of color words to get you started.

- **Blond:** white blond, cream, blond, flax, yellow blond, honey, taupe, deep taupe, ash blond, dark blond
- **Brown:** golden brown, mahogany, cool dark brown, ash brown, deep ash brown, charcoal brown, dark brown
- **Black:** off black, brown black, blue black
- **Red:** strawberry blond, carrot, rust, red, auburn
- **Gray:** golden gray, dove gray, pearl, cool gray, silver gray, charcoal, silver
- **White:** white, oyster, platinum

8. *Keep noticing.* You'll be using your new sensitized vision to identify the colors that best express who you are, so you'll need to keep your eyes open! Like anything else, sharp vision takes practice, so continue to notice the colors of your world. Focus especially on identifying the subtle tones of your skin, eyes, and hair. When you come to identify the specific colors that are unique to you, you'll be amazed at how your new clear vision leads you to make both unexpected and flattering choices. (You'll have a chance to choose these colors in the next three chapters.)

SHOW SOME EMOTION

In this chapter, I asked you to become superobjective about viewing, first some produce, then yourself, as objectively as possible. For the rest of the book, however, we'll be focusing on how color evokes emotion and how it expresses deep aspects of your personality and spirit. Like Lizzie and my actress client, you'll come to understand how showing up in your true colors is the key to holding everything you want in the palm of your hand—along with the essence, romantic, and dramatic colors that you will find there!

2

three colors that can change your life:

identifying your essence, romantic, and dramatic colors

once you understand the power of your **true colors,** you won't just want to wear them—you'll want to surround yourself with them! Even though my primary role is as a stylist and costume designer, I often find myself working with clients who want to extend the principles of *true color* and *authentic style* into their homes and offices.

One such client was Camilla, who became so enthusiastic about the *true colors* in her wardrobe that she chose them for every room in her home as well. She was particularly proud of her home office, where she'd had the walls painted bright blueberry with a striking vanilla trim. Camilla fit the *Archetype* that I call Vital Spring, or the Prom Queen, a fun-loving, charismatic woman whose *authentic style* was wonderfully expressed in bright, clear colors. Every client who entered the newly painted room praised the colors—how bright and cheerful they were, how unusual, how uplifting.

The only problem was, Camilla was a therapist and her clients were the people who had come to her for help. The brilliant blueberry happened to be her *dramatic* color—the power color that makes people sit up and take notice—but it wasn't a shade that inspired comfort or trust or intimacy. Camilla's clients admired the room and maybe they even enjoyed it, but it didn't evoke the response she was looking for.

When Camilla came to me with this new concern, I thought for a while. "Maybe we should paint that office in your *essence* color," I finally suggested.

As we've seen, the *dramatic* color is the hue taken from the shade of your veins that reveals your power, your charisma, and your sense of authority. That makes it the color you wear to make a strong impression, perhaps on a job interview, for a presentation, or at a party where you want to network with lots of powerful people. You might also choose it for a room in which you plan to entertain, putting everyone on notice that this is a room in which exciting, dramatic events take place: *Here* is where the party is!

The *essence* color, by contrast, is the color that harmonizes your skin tones and reveals your most genuine, open, and essential self. This shade is far more quiet and vulnerable than your *dramatic* color—in fact, it's downright intimate. Wearing a garment in your *essence* color suggests that you have allowed yourself to be revealed, and that you are open to others revealing themselves as well. It almost suggests a kind of nakedness—not in a sexual or sensual way, but as a heartfelt gift, a way of offering your authentic, undisguised self. Painting a room in your *essence* color can have a similar effect. Instead of "Here is where the party is!" you're saying, "Here is a place where we can be honest and open with one another."

Camilla looked at the paint chips I had brought to our meeting, turning her *essence* color over and over in her hand. The *essence* color can be a wide range of colors, shades of pink, beige, yellow, gold, olive, or brown. Camilla's *essence* color was a warm, soft peach. It didn't exactly match her skin—which, as we've seen, has many different tones. Instead, it harmonized and smoothed the different skin shades into one subtle, glowing color.

"Sure," she said, holding the chip next to her hand, appreciating its gentle warmth. "Let's give it a try."

Three months later, Camilla called to give me an update. "Your idea was inspired," she said bluntly. "In fact, I'm a little overwhelmed. People who walk into that room don't comment on the color—I'm not sure they even notice it, consciously—but somehow it affects them. It must. Because my clients are opening up more quickly and more fully than ever before—it's kind of unbelievable."

I asked Camilla how she thought the room had affected her clients, and in true therapist style, she considered my question for a few minutes before replying.

"You know," she said finally, "I think there's some way that using my *essence* color—my skin tone—just makes me more available somehow. It's as though I'm saying, 'Here I am, no pretense, no cover-ups, nothing to hide, nothing to fake. This is who *I* am. Now, who are *you*?'"

I tried to imagine Camilla sitting in her *essence*-colored office, the color of the walls almost like an extension of herself, and even just picturing the effect, I had to smile. "It's as though you're being vulnerable to your clients and giving them a hug at the same time," I suggested.

"Yes!" Camilla agreed. "That's it exactly."

LOVE THE SKIN YOU'RE IN

As we've seen, skin tones are a key element in your true colors, helping to determine your **essence, romantic,** and **dramatic** colors. When you can identify these colors, you can begin to choose the colors, clothes, and objects that reveal your true self. You can begin to create not only a wardrobe but a warm, welcoming home environment and a stimulating, nurturing office to serve your most basic needs: for self-expression, passion, and power.

> **Your *True Colors***
>
> **Essence Color:** The color that harmonizes your skin tones and reveals your most genuine, open, and essential self; your version of white; wear it when you are having an intimate conversation, when you are meditating, or when you want to be completely open and honest.

REVEALING YOUR TRUE SELF: YOUR *ESSENCE* COLOR

As Camilla learned, your *essence* color expresses your most basic self. It helps you find comfort, a way to cope, and the place to ground yourself. If you need to get back to your center, your essence color leads you there. If you want to remind yourself of that primal inner self, untouched by outside influences, your essence color will help you remember. And if you want to express that basic, inner self to the rest of the world, your essence color is where you start.

Your *essence* color is not a single exact match of your skin—how could it be? As we've already seen, your skin holds many different tones and shades, and no one color could match them all. Rather, an *essence* color sets off all of the other colors. When you hold it beside your hand or your face, your *essence* color makes all the other colors look blended and harmonious rather than blotchy, pale, sallow, or simply dull. When you place your true *essence* color beside your skin, your skin glows.

FIND YOUR *ESSENCE* COLOR

Try one or more of these options to discover the color that harmonizes your skin tones and makes your skin glow.

1. **Paint chips.** When I work with clients, this is what I use. Go to the paint store or the hardware store and buy a set of paint chips that seem to resemble the skin tones found in your hand. Then, in a comfortable place with natural light, hold up each chip to your skin and find

> **HINT:** Your *essence* color should be very close to the dominant tone in your skin, but it will somehow seem to incorporate and bring out all the other tones as well.

   the one that gives your skin the smoothing effect. Remember, you're looking for the color that harmonizes your skin, pulling all the different colors together.
2. **Lingerie.** Often, lingerie is made in *essence* tones. You might not be able to find a sufficiently wide range of lingerie, but give it a try—you might luck out!
3. **Foundation makeup.** You might also try to find a foundation that harmonizes the colors of your skin. Again, you're not looking for an exact match but the color that makes all your different skin tones

come together—the shade that, when you hold it beside your skin, makes your skin look glowing and smooth.

4. *Makeup consultant.* While you're at the makeup counter, you might ask the makeover expert for help in locating the right shade for you. I'm not suggesting that you necessarily have to wear foundation makeup, but you can use the shade you identify to help you select garments and accessories.

Creating Your Authentic Style: Look for your essence color in the nearby box and note it below.

My *Essence* Color *(my version of WHITE)*:

Possible Candidates for Your *Essence* Colors (or find your own names for these colors)

Whites: milky white, porcelain, creamy ivory, bisque, parchment, pearl

Pinks: cream with an undertone of peach or rose; cameo, seashell, cool pink, ice pink, dusty rose, violet rose, peach, peach pink

Yellows: yellow brown, yellow beige, sand

Golds: honey, golden beige, golden brown, olive gold, golden tan

Beiges: pale beige, rose beige, greige (grayish beige), copper beige, tawny beige, brown beige

Browns: olive, rose brown, gray brown, mahogany, chestnut, toasted golden brown, cedar, caramel, bronze, ash, blue black

Open Up to Your *Essence* Color

You don't have to wait until it's time to go shopping to discover the profound ways your essence color can affect your mood and your environment. Get to know your essence color by trying out the following suggestions:

1. *Find a lamp with a shade in this color.* You can read by this light or simply switch it on when you want some quiet time to yourself. The illumination of the shade will cast a soft light that is particularly becoming and supportive of you.

2. *Meditate or do yoga in essence-colored clothes.* This is especially effective if you're in the privacy of your own home. Nothing feels lighter to wear than your *essence* color, which comes to seem like an extension of your own skin. If you're working out in front of a mirror, wearing nothing but your *essence* color frees you to concentrate on yourself and your breathing—it seems that there is nothing else to look at! (If you've ever done your yoga practice in the nude, you already know what this feels like!)

3. *Choose your essence color as the background for your business card.* Then, when you hand someone your card, it will seem like a warm and friendly extension of yourself.

4. *Paint your bedroom this color.* Every morning when you wake up, you will feel warm, easy, and vulnerable yet supported. If you really want to cocoon, carpet your bedroom floor in this color as well. You've now created the ultimate refuge for a sleep-in day! And if you share your bedroom or choose to invite

someone into it, your *essence* color signals that you are sharing your most intimate and authentic self—and invites your partner to do so as well.

5. ***Buy yourself a soft robe in this color.*** After a trying day, putting on the robe will seem like the perfect way to feel as though you're back in your own skin.

Your *True Colors*

Romantic **Color:** The color reflected by your flushed skin, which reveals your passion, your sexual energy, and your romantic self; your version of *red*; wear it on a hot date, a romantic evening, or any time you want your passion to show.

OPENING YOUR HEART: YOUR *ROMANTIC* COLOR

Your essence color is only one of the three colors inspired by the coloring in your skin. The second is your romantic color. While your essence color expresses your innermost spirit, your romantic color expresses your passion, your sexuality, and your heart.

Your own personal version of red, your *romantic* color is taken from your flushed skin, evoking the vitality of the blood that flows through your arteries. This is the color that reveals your passion, your sexual energy, and your romantic self, so wear it on a hot date or a romantic outing with your significant other. Wear it as well for a warm, loving evening with friends; to make a relaxed, personal connection with a valued client or colleague; or to reconnect with your own joie de vivre, your fun-loving side, and your "heart energy." You can get this effect whether you use your *romantic* color as an accent, such as a blouse or scarf, or as an entire outfit, such as a dress or suit. As you can see from the box below, the color that expresses your passion and love might indeed be red—but it might also be tangerine, fuchsia, coral, rust, or even mahogany.

FIND YOUR *ROMANTIC* COLOR

Follow these steps to discover the color that evokes your flushed skin and shows your warmest, most passionate self:

1. In natural light, hold your hand over a white piece of paper with your palm facing you. Curl your fingers so that your palm is "cupped."
2. Look carefully at the most flushed areas of your palm and notice the shade.
3. Now, place a finger on each side of the fingerprint of your index finger and pinch your finger. What is the color of your flushed skin? (This is also the color that your ears might turn when very hot or cold.)
4. Look in the bottom of your palm on the side closest to your little finger.
5. If your palm includes deeper shades that make it difficult to see this color, you might want to hold your hand next to your gums. The contrast will help bring out the different shades in your palm.

Creating Your Authentic Style: Look for your romantic color in the nearby box and note the group in which it appears. Write the romantic color and the letter of its group in the spaces below.

My *Romantic* Color *(my version of RED)*:

_____

My Letter: _____

Possible Candidates for Your *Romantic* Color

A. **Crisp and Clear:** Barbie doll pink, cool dusty pink, carnation, peach, peach coral, light orange, Creamsicle, apricot, clear red, bright cherry, bright coral

B. **Cool and Relaxed:** cool shell pink, rose pink, dusty rose, strawberry, raspberry, watermelon, geranium, fuchsia, burgundy, rusty burgundy, mulberry, claret, cranberry, maroon

C. **Warm and Mellow:** coral pink, salmon, tangerine, deep apricot, burnt peach, flame, orange red, tomato, Chinese red, Christmas red, cayenne, terra-cotta, paprika, brick red, cinnamon, Indian red brown, rust

D. **Rich and Contrasted:** ballet pink, shocking pink, dusted fuchsia, magenta, poppy, ruby, fire engine red, crimson, scarlet, vermilion, blue red, cranberry, dark cherry, rusty brick, port

HINT: Once you've identified your *romantic* color, you might go to the lipstick counter and choose a lipstick that matches it. You can wear your *romantic* lipstick or gloss, and you can also take it with you when you shop and use it to match fabrics and accessories.

SEVEN WAYS TO MAKE FRIENDS WITH
YOUR *ROMANTIC* COLOR

There are many ways to surround yourself with this warm, energizing color. Here are a few suggestions:

1. ***Put it on your dinner table***—use as an accent in placemats, a tablecloth, a centerpiece, or napkin rings. Your warm, hearty *romantic* color will remind

your dinner companions that when you serve food, it's a gift from the heart.

2. *Wrap a gift in it.* You might even make it your signature gift wrap for a loving way to give a present.

3. *Buy a pen or stationery in that color.* Then write a love note or a letter to a friend. For extra credit, make valentines in this color!

4. *Find a flower or an ornament in this color for your desk at work.* When you're tired, just a glance at your *romantic* color can give you a cheering energy boost.

5. *Buy a piece of art—or even a postcard—featuring this color.* You'll find that your *romantic* color inspires you—and it will warm up any space you inhabit, even an office.

6. *Buy some lingerie, a nightgown, a robe, or a chemise in this color.* If you're not yet ready to wear your version of red in public, why not wear it in private? You'll soon discover how romantic and alive your *romantic* color makes you feel.

7. *Wear jewelry in that color.* If you can find natural stones in your *romantic* color, so much the better. Vibrations from stones or crystals of your *romantic* color can be very healing.

Your *True Colors*

Dramatic **Color:** The color taken from the shade of your veins, which shows your power, your charisma, and your sense of authority; your version of *blue*; wear it on a job interview, for a formal presentation, or any time you want to make a strong impression.

Expressing Your Power: Your *Dramatic* Color

Last but definitely not least, your skin holds a third color you should know about: your dramatic color. True to its name, your dramatic color makes a strong, dramatic impression as it reveals your power, your charisma, and your sense of authority. The strongest contrast to your natural coloring, your dramatic color is your version of blue (though for some of you, that "blue" might appear as a shade of green or purple).

You'd wear your *dramatic* color—either as an accent or as an entire outfit—to a job interview, a formal party, or a key presentation—any occasion on which you want to "take the stage" as the center of attention. Because of its strong, outwardly directed energy, it's also a good color for formfitting active wear, such as bathing suits, ski outfits, and workout clothes. On the other hand, you probably won't want to sport this intense color when you're tired or trying to relax in loose-fitting clothing.

If you're wondering how your *dramatic* color could change your life, try wearing yours the next time you need to make a strong, long-lasting impression, such as hosting a charity fundraiser, attending a high school reunion, or even posing for a driver's license photo. You might be surprised at the result!

Find Your *Dramatic* Color

Follow these steps to discover the color that provides the strongest contrast to your natural coloring and shows your most powerful, charismatic, and authoritative self:

1. In natural light, hold your hand so you can see the veins below your wrist. Locate the vein that's most pronounced.

2. Identify the darkest color you can see in your veins; the shade of blue, green, or purple that offers the highest contrast to the other elements of your coloring. This is your most *dramatic* color.

3. Go on to identify another two shades of blue, green, or purple that you can find in your veins. You can also wear these as milder, less intense versions of your *dramatic* color.

Creating Your Authentic Style: Look for your dramatic color in the box below and note the group in which it appears. Look ONLY at the group beside the letter that you identified for your romantic color.

My *Dramatic* Color *(my version of BLUE)*:

_____

My Letter: _____

Possible Candidates for Your *Dramatic* Color

A. Light: Kelly green, shamrock, vivid jade, turquoise green, aqua, clear turquoise, robin's egg blue, ultramarine, cerulean, cornflower blue, pacific blue, electric blue, blueberry, bluebell, periwinkle, pansy, wisteria, lilac, clear violet

B. Mixed: frosted wintergreen, English holly, clear emerald, evergreen, spruce, cool spruce, robin's egg green, aquamarine, deep sky blue, Wedgwood, Danube blue, deep sapphire, blue violet, powdered periwinkle, hyacinth, lavender, blackberry, amethyst, plum, violet

C. Deep: deep fern, cypress, seaweed green, Persian green, evergreen, dark emerald, jade, turquoise green, peacock green, sea green, deep teal, peacock blue,

> turquoise blue, lapis blue, Egyptian blue, Nile blue,
> Venetian blue
>
> **D. Bold:** wintergreen, green pea, juniper, Viridian green,
> racing green, pine, ocean green, cool jade, emerald,
> peacock, deep blue green, clear sapphire, cobalt blue,
> royal blue, Persian indigo, royal purple, eggplant, black
> plum, periwinkle dust
>
> **HINT:** Once you've identified your *dramatic* color, find an
> eye shadow that matches it exactly. Then take this eye shadow
> with you when you shop, to check against your garments and
> accessories.

Creating Your Authentic Style: Note the letter that appeared beside your romantic color. Look for that letter in the following list and circle the word beside it. That is your Season.

My Season is:

a) Spring
b) Summer
c) Autumn
d) Winter

CELEBRATE YOURSELF WITH YOUR *DRAMATIC* COLOR

You can use your dramatic color to celebrate yourself in public by purchasing a ski ensemble in it or even purchasing a car in the exact shade. But you can also celebrate yourself in more private and subtle ways; for example:

1. Find some folders or binders in this color, and when you're starting a project or making a presentation, package it in your *dramatic* color for extra *oomph*!

2. Choose a frame for a photo on your desk, and then look at it or hold it when you're making an important call or writing up a big presentation. This color helps you say to yourself, "I'm onstage. I'm important, look at me!"

3. Buy a scarf in this color and then put it on at the end of a long, draining day, especially when you have to go out and make a good impression on someone that evening. The invigorating power of your *dramatic* color will rev you up in no time!

4. Decorate the entryway to your home in this color, especially if you entertain a lot. Your *dramatic* color says, "Hey, here's my home! Look, the entertainment is about to begin!"

5. Buy a bicycle or exercise bike in this color. You will feel energized and ready to pedal fast!

6. Buy napkins, coasters, or dessert plates in this color, and use them to make a big, dramatic splash whenever you have guests over.

7. Buy rain boots in this color. Adding a touch of drama is always good for perking up a rainy day.

8. Buy some jewelry in this color and wear it when you need to bring a touch of authority to the encounter. Great for, say, a parent-teacher meeting or an important talk with your boss.

9. Decorate your windowsill at home or at work with glass bottles or a glass art piece in this color. When the sun lights up your *dramatic* color, it makes you the star!

10. Buy a wineglass in this color—and save it for making toasts to yourself! After all, who else but you should be lauded as the star of your own life story?

GETTING TO KNOW YOUR *ESSENCE*, *ROMANTIC*, AND *DRAMATIC* COLORS

By the time you've finished this book, you'll be putting together outfits that rely on your essence, romantic, and dramatic colors. But you don't have to wait till then. Experiment with wearing these colors in the form of a blouse, a scarf, a pair of shorts. See how you feel when you dress yourself in these shades or how it affects you when a bath towel, candle, or ornament brings these colors into your life. The more you understand about your own response to these colors, the better you'll be able to use them in your palette.

So have fun! Think of these colors as new kids on the playground. You don't have to become best friends right away. Just start the getting-to-know-you process—and read on to meet some more new colors.

Creating Your Authentic Style: Keep track of the discoveries you've made in this chapter by filling out the following chart:

My *Essence* Color *(my version of white)*:
_____

My *Romantic* Color *(my version of red)*:
_____

My *Dramatic* Color *(my version of blue)*:
_____

My Season: _____

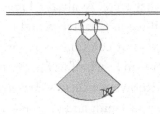

3

color me energized:

finding your energy and tranquil colors

few years ago, I was invited to redesign the offices of a subsidized project for formerly homeless families in Cleveland. This unusual and very inspiring agency included two social workers whose job was to help the tenants with any problem that came up, from dealing with the Department of Social Services to coping with family crises.

I was full of admiration for the long hours and profound dedication of the tiny staff, but I could see immediately that both women were suffering from a bad case of burnout. The daily workload was demanding enough, but when I saw where the work was being done, I marveled that they hadn't given up in despair. Cold, dingy, and dirty white, lit by harsh fluorescent light and assaulted by the incessant traffic noise from the adjacent street, the work space was one of the most dismal I had ever seen. It was a striking example of how color, light, and overall style can create—or kill—positive energy.

The staff was moving into new offices across the street, and a foundation had donated a modest sum to redecorate them. My first move was to meet with the social workers and get some sense of who they were. As always, I relied on my clients' *Archetypes*. As we'll see in Chapters 5 and 6, every one of us has a *Season* based on our coloring—you discovered yours in the previous chapter—and each of us fits one of six *Archetypes* within our *Season*. Knowing a client's *Archetype* helps me key in on her personality and spirit and gives me a more complete understanding of the ways that color can support, inspire, and reveal her true self.

I quickly realized that Jolene was a Soft Winter, fitting the *Archetype* of the Romantic Poetess. True to her *Archetype,* she possessed a deep, inner well of spirituality and truth, but she was also hypersensitive to anything harsh, jarring, or out of tune.

Her coworker, Carmen, was a Classic Summer, fitting the *Archetype* of the Classic Beauty. Carmen was the kind of person who only had to walk through the door to brighten a room and lift everybody's spirits. But she herself needed to be surrounded by warm, harmonious colors that provided her with the "sunlight" she needed to grow.

Your *True Colors*

Energy **Color:** The color seen in the darkest part of your iris (not the ring outside the iris—you'll be using that for your First Base), which taps into the deepest sources of your energy; helps you restore and balance your energy; wear it when you want to be calm, self-possessed, and centered, such as at a family reunion, a meeting with your child's teacher, or a corporate retreat.

> **Tranquil Color:** The color found in the lightest part of your iris, which taps into the deepest sources of your tranquility; helps you relax and release stress; wear it when you want to recover from a challenging situation, such as after a long day at work.

After talking with the women at length, I decided that these women should have their offices painted in their *energy* colors. Taken from the darkest color in the iris, your *energy* color taps into the deepest sources of your energy and helps you restore and balance your energy.

Because this color expresses the depths of your spirit, it is often the fastest route to connecting to your own inner reserves of strength and serenity.

I often think that each of your *true colors* has its own persona. The *essence* color represents the pure "naked self," the *romantic* is the "sexy siren," and the *dramatic* color is the "guest of honor." The *energy* color though, has a dual personality: It is the "nurturer" but also the "nurtured," feeding and supporting both you and the people in your presence. I envision your *energy* color as a soft hand laid against the small of your back, supporting you even as it gently urges you forward. It seemed like the perfect choice to both calm and invigorate these two heroic women in their grueling but rewarding work.

Each woman was fortunate to have a tiny adjoining bathroom beside her office, and for these rooms I chose their *tranquil* colors. The *tranquil* color is also taken from the eye, but from the lightest shade in the iris. As the name suggests, your *tranquil* color taps into the deepest sources of your tranquility, helping you relax and release stress. If the *energy* color is the "nurturer/nurtured," the *tranquil* color is "the mellow self," the self you show the world after you have released all your tension and restored your serenity.

My hope was that the *energy* colors in the offices would help direct the women's energy outward, toward their clients, while still helping them recharge their batteries for each new client. The *tranquil* bathrooms, on the other hand, would cue them to direct their energy inward, taking that private time to replenish their inner stores of hope, faith, and strength.

And so it came to pass! Jolene loved her pine green office and gray-green bathroom, and Carmen was equally thrilled with her slate blue office and dusty lavender bathroom. In fact, when each woman walked into her new rooms, you could actually see her relax, almost as though she were absorbing waves of calming energy from the surrounding colors.

Although both women had been considering moves to another agency, they each elected to remain at the housing project. Their supervisor was relieved to keep such dedicated workers, and I was humbled to discover yet another example of the healing power of color.

An Eye for Color

In this chapter, we'll explore two of your true colors: your energy color and your tranquil color. In a way, these two colors seem like polar opposites: The first one matches your energy, while the second calms you down. In another way, though, your energy and your tranquil colors are intimately related. After all, one comes from the deepest shades of your iris while the other comes from your lightest eye tones.

Understanding these two colors allows you to unlock your inner resources in a whole new way, sustaining and supporting your energy throughout the day while maintaining your serenity and calm. Knowing about these **true colors** also enables you to display other aspects of yourself, showing loved ones and coworkers your energetic and tranquil sides, both of which can create the impression of effortless, artless appeal.

OPENING TO YOUR INNER SELF: YOUR *ENERGY* COLOR

A flattering effect is easily achieved by wearing your energy color. This supportive shade blends with your energy and takes very little effort to wear. It is carried off for any occasion in any sort of clothing, including suits, dresses, sweaters, trousers, and skirts.

Because your **energy** color matches your own energy, you feel restored and comforted when you wear or surround yourself with these tones. You never get tired of your **energy** color, which is flattering in any setting. Because of its versatility, it is also good for travel. And because of its healing, calming effect, your **energy** color is useful to wear when trying to resolve a conflict, smooth ruffled feathers, or bring a disagreement to a happy conclusion.

FIND YOUR *ENERGY* COLOR

1. Take a look in a mirror, a magnifying mirror if possible, in natural, indirect light. If you can, remove any garments that are visible in the mirror, so that all you can see are your eyes and skin, with no other colors to distract you.

2. As you did with your skin, notice how many different colors, shades, and tones are in your eyes. You may be used to thinking of them as simply "blue" or "brown," but blue eyes might also include tones of

gray, ice blue, blue white, or pale green, while brown eyes might include touches of olive, gold, topaz, or red brown. Let your eye linger on its own reflection and notice how much more you can see once you allow yourself to really look.

3. Remember, the colors you're looking for may not be terribly obvious, especially with brown eyes. If you're having trouble identifying the many different subtle colors in your iris, you can give yourself some help by holding different shades of blue, green, orange, yellow, and purple next to your eye. These adjacent colors will help bring out shades that you might otherwise have to struggle to discern.

4. When you've seen all you can, zero in on the darkest part of your iris, but not the ring around your iris (you'll be using the dark ring around your iris to identify your version of black, your First Base neutral). That dark part *within* your iris is your *energy* color.

Possible Candidates for Your *Energy* Color

Purples: dusty orchid, pale violet

Blues and Grays: light gray, ice blue, blue quartz, denim, smoky teal, pale aqua, anthracite

Greens: green quartz, English ivy, sage, julep, pine, green tourmaline, verde, Irish green, moss, army green, asparagus, leaf, stem green, green grape, lime, electric green, tropical green, grass, green apple, parrot, green pear, chartreuse, green curry

Yellows and Golds: yellow pear, marigold, orange sherbet, toasted pumpkin, tiger's eye, tarnished brass, sap, brown tourmaline, smoky topaz

Creating Your Authentic Style: Complete the exercise above and identify your energy color.

My *Energy* Color: _____

OPEN UP TO POSSIBILITY: YOUR *ENERGY* COLOR

Since your energy color matches your own inner energy, it's great to wear for challenging situations. Wearing your energy color will keep you in touch with your true self while reminding others of who you really are. Here are some occasions on which wearing your energy color can serve you well:

1. *Time with your child.* When you spend time with your child, often, your primary goal is to listen—to be there for anything your kid may feel like sharing with you about his or her life. If you want to be receptive on such an occasion, your *dramatic* color may make you a bit too dominant, while your *tranquil* color, as we'll see, may make you appear too laid-back. Your *essence* color might be an option, but it might make you *too* vulnerable, turning you into your child's equal instead of the parental figure that children also need. The solution? Try a sweater, a pair of slacks, or even a jacket in your *energy* color. It will give you support for hearing any secrets your son or daughter has to share, even as it reminds your child of how open and available you are. But it also lets you maintain a healthy amount of distance and self-possession, which your child will appreciate.

2. *A blind date.* If you've already met your evening's partner, you might want to go with your *romantic* color, which brings your passionate, sexual nature to

the surface. But if you have no idea who'll show up at that restaurant, maybe your *energy* color would be a better choice. While your *essence* color is simple and flattering, it may be a bit too vulnerable to meet a stranger in. The *energy* color, though, reveals a woman who is open to possibilities without pre-determining how the evening is going to go. Instead of putting your sexual side in the foreground, you're putting the focus on who you are—and what better way to get to know a new person than that?

3. *A corporate retreat.* You might want to show up for work in your *dramatic* color, trying to achieve that *kaboom* effect to impress your boss or a powerful coworker. Or if you've got a crush on a coworker, your *romantic* color might do the trick. At a corporate retreat, though, you're supposed to "come as you are." Your *energy* color reinforces the idea that you're showing up to listen as well as to participate, without focusing on either your power or your sexuality. "I'm ready to listen, absorb—and give back," this color proclaims, revealing your self without being selfish.

4. *A visit with a friend who needs support.* If you're trying to cheer or comfort a friend who's going through a divorce, struggling with an illness, or coping with family problems, your *energy* color helps you rise to the occasion with quiet, steady support. Wearing a sweater or jacket in your *energy* color makes a clear, helpful statement: "I'm here, ready for whatever you need. I'm showing up for you."

5. *A gathering with family or in-laws.* We may love our families, but let's face it: Sometimes they make

it difficult for us to stay in touch with our best and truest selves. A blouse, shirt, or pair of *energy*-colored slacks can help you break through the family myths and in-law wishes to remind yourself of who you *really* are.

TUNING IN TO YOUR SERENITY: YOUR *TRANQUIL* COLOR

My client Alys was getting married and she couldn't have been happier. A skilled practitioner of the Alexander Technique, she was a lovely pink-beige–skinned, cornflower blue–eyed ash blonde, a nurturing woman who embodied the Earth Mother of her Dusky Summer Archetype. She and her Danish husband were planning to settle in Ireland and they'd chosen a tiny country chapel in a little village for their upcoming wedding.

Alys and Karl both had relatives who had settled in various countries around the world, and their large, extended families were viewing the event as a kind of glorified family reunion. Invitations had gone out to two mothers, several sisters, and a couple dozen aunts and cousins, every one of whom seemed to have a strong opinion about what these nuptials needed to be. Alys's mother wanted her daughter to wear her old wedding dress, while Alys's future mother-in-law had ideas about the flowers and the wedding supper. Alys's older sister, the matron of honor, refused to wear blue; Alys's new sister-in-law wanted Alys to wear a train so that her little girl could carry it down the aisle; Karl's aunt Helle insisted that no Jensen family wedding would be complete without the evergreen decorations that had become a family tradition, and so on.

"Isn't this supposed to be *my* wedding?" Alys asked me wryly. "They're not even making suggestions anymore—everyone is insisting that I do it *her* way. Look, I love my family—I even love Karl's family! I want every one of them there. But this has got to feel like *my* day—*our* day—or we'll both feel dreadfully cheated."

"So you're not looking for the white dress with the long train?" I said tentatively. I certainly didn't want my voice to be one more added to the clamor.

Alys shuddered. "Heavens no," she said. "Both our mothers did that whole white-dress-and-seven-bridesmaids thing. Karl and I want to start our own tradition."

I thought for a minute. I had been working with Alys for a while, first identifying her **true colors,** then going on several shopping trips with her. She had mastered the elements of her **authentic style** and by this time, she had truly become her own stylist. I knew she'd take seriously whatever suggestions I made, but I also knew that she was now ready to bring her own opinions to the table.

"You could wear a dress in your **essence** color," I suggested. After all our work together, Alys already knew that the **essence** color harmonizes the skin tone, almost as though you're clothed in a second skin. But she shook her head.

"Too vulnerable," she said succinctly. "At some point, one of them is going to ask me why I'm not serving the traditional eight-course meal that Uncle Alfie had at *his* wedding, and I'm going to need every ounce of strength to just smile and shake my head."

"Maybe your **romantic** color?" I offered. After all, the **romantic** color embodies passion, emotion, and romance. Although it's a version of red rather than the traditional white, it could make a strong statement about Alys and Karl's feelings for each other.

But Alys shook her head again. "Too stimulating," she said. "I want to calm these people down, not rev them up. Hey, they're driving me insane—I want to calm *myself* down. I just want to look at myself in a beautiful dress and think about my wonderful man and be happy. I don't want to look like I'm trying to steam-roll anybody—and I couldn't do it anyway; all of them together are just too powerful. Besides, the last thing I want on my wedding day is to have to work. I just want to be calm. And I want all of them to become calm, simply by looking at me."

"Well, then, we're talking about your *tranquil* color," I said. "That's the most calming color in your palette—your 'spa color,' remember? And yours is a lovely soft green that should make a beautiful wedding dress."

Alys looked at me thoughtfully. "Yes," she said slowly. "My tranquil color . . . that might work. Maybe for Karl, too—maybe he could wear his tranquil color in a tie."

As we discussed the idea further, we both grew enthusiastic. "I want to give everyone there a hug," Alys said ruefully, "because honestly, I do love them. If I didn't, we wouldn't invite them, we would've eloped. But there's all this raging emotion—we've got to take it down a notch!"

Later, when Alys e-mailed me the wedding photos, I saw that her dress was a beautiful peau de soie tea dress in a gorgeous pastel shade of ivy green. The color hit the right note exactly: relaxed, serene, welcoming, at peace. Theirs was an afternoon wedding, just before sunset, when the light was mellow and soft, and both Alys and her bridegroom looked happy and secure. I was happy, too, that we'd been able to make such good use of the soothing, calming properties of her *tranquil* color.

FIND YOUR *TRANQUIL* COLOR

1. Take a look in a mirror, a magnifying mirror if possible. Again, observe yourself in natural, indirect light.

If you can, remove any garments that are visible in the mirror, so that all you can see is your eyes and skin, with no other colors to distract you.

2. As you did when searching for your *energy* color, notice as many different shades and tones within your iris as you can. And, as before, if you need to give your vision a boost, hold different shades of blue, green, orange, yellow, and purple next to your eye, so that the contrasts and reflections can help you see colors you might otherwise not notice.

3. Finally settle on the lightest area of your iris. That's your *tranquil* color.

Possible Candidates for Your *Tranquil* Color

Purples: dusty lilac, wisteria, pale blue violet

Blues: Alice blue, chambray blue, blue gray, slate blue, robin's egg blue, dusty teal

Greens: jade green, mint, thistle, fern, moon green, spring green, celadon, celery, aloe, parakeet, brassy green

Yellows and Golds: old gold, chartreuse yellow, lemon chiffon, banana, corn, school bus yellow, mustard, goldenrod

Browns: bronze, raw umber, rust brown, amber, maple, copper

Creating Your Authentic Style: Complete the exercise above and identify your tranquil color.

My *Tranquil* Color: _____

Relax with Your *Tranquil* Color

You may or may not choose this color for your wedding dress! But you can still discover the healing power of color by tuning into the shade that expresses your own personal "spa energy." When you want to let go of tension and reconnect to your sense of calm, you can wear tranquil-colored clothes—or try one of the following suggestions:

1. Buy yourself a cashmere throw in this color—it will seem cozy, warm, and comforting.
2. Choose a comfy pair of slippers in your *tranquil* color. Let your feet be tranquil, too!
3. Put a *tranquil*-colored scented candle by your bed or bathtub. Both the color and the aroma will help you relax.
4. Choose patio glassware in this color to make your time outdoors more soothing and refreshing.
5. Find a plant that includes your *tranquil* color and put it anywhere you'd like to unwind: in your bedroom, in the TV room, even by your desk at work if you want to access your serene side from time to time.
6. Use this "spa color" to paint your bathroom, to choose your towels, or to monogram your towels. Every bath and shower can become a chance to de-stress.
7. Buy toiletries and soaps in your *tranquil* color, for a dose of serenity during the day.
8. Choose an umbrella in this color, and feel yourself relax under its *tranquil* protection.
9. Purchase some jewelry or a scarf in your *tranquil* color and wear it on difficult occasions. Whether you're coping with your mother-in-law or with

your boss, your *tranquil* color can help you remind
yourself of who you really are!

10. Buy a brush or hand mirror in your *tranquil* color,
so that every time you brush your hair or check
your makeup, you're tapping into tranquility and
peace.

THE HEALING POWER OF COLOR

I love working with *energy* and *tranquil* colors because they
have such an extraordinary effect on our emotions, mood, and
sense of well-being. You may be ready to run right out and buy
a few "spa" outfits in your *tranquil* color—or you may still be
preparing yourself to implement these principles in your wardrobe. Either way, I invite you to notice the powerful effects that
your *energy* and *tranquil* colors can have on you and to experiment with different ways of bringing these colors into your life.
I promise you, you'll be glad you did!

Creating Your Authentic Style: Keep track of the discoveries
you've made in this chapter by filling out the following chart:

My *Energy* Color: _____

My *Tranquil* Color: _____

4

getting to third base:

choosing your versions of black, brown, and khaki

nOW that you've identified the colors that best express the facets of your spirit—your **essence, romantic, dramatic, energy,** and **tranquil** colors—it's time to get back to basics. Literally. This chapter is where I'll show you how to choose the three "neutral" **base** colors that you can use to build your wardrobe, your versions of black, brown, and khaki.

As you've already seen by now, these may not actually *be* black, brown, or khaki. For some women, yes, the classic versions of these hues are indeed their **true colors.** But other women express themselves differently. For Anne Hathaway, "black" may be a mid-tone gray, while Meredith Vieira's "black" is actually prune. Your "brown" might range from chocolate to rust to gunmetal, or it might be any one of a hundred other shades; while your "khaki" could be beige, olive green, or even dove gray. So in this chapter, I'll show you how to use your hair and eye colors to identify your three **base** colors: your own personal versions of black, brown, and khaki. I'll also help you figure out how to combine your **bases** with the other colors we've explored to create formal, somewhat less formal, and downright casual outfits.

GOING POSITIVE WITH YOUR NEUTRALS

At first glance, neutral colors don't really "do" anything. No one will say, "Wow, that outfit really brings out your eyes" when you're wearing your version of black, or "I've never seen your skin glow like that" when you're wearing your version of brown. Instead, neutrals are like the bare wall behind the portrait—the blank space that sets off your lovely face and your animated spirit. Neutrals don't bring the drama—but they do provide the very best backdrop against which the drama can take place.

Another way to think about neutrals is to remember that they don't express your personality—so the less personality you want to express in a situation, the more you rely on them. That's why wearing black is so often used for uniforms: The wearer's own personality is submerged into the role he or she is asked to perform. So if you'd like to fade into the background at a corporate gathering or family get-together, try showing up in a neutral color.

On the other hand, choosing a neutral background for one fabulously colored piece—a scarf, some big earrings, a necklace, or a hat—is a great way to set off a brilliant accessory and a terrific way to make a neutral suit do multiple duty as the background to a parade of striking scarves, jewelry, and other adornments in one of your five **true colors.** Let the single striking accessory express your personality through your **essence**-colored pink-beige scarf, your **romantic** garnet earrings, or a *dramatic* string of purple glass beads. Then allow the rest of your outfit to recede into the background by choosing one of your *three bases* for your dress, suit, or sweater and slacks.

As we'll see in Chapter 9, one of the best ways to save money with your wardrobe is to get one basic piece in each *base* and then add a blouse, sweater, or shell in one of your five colors. For example, a "black" suit with an *essence*-colored blouse offers just a touch of vulnerability, while a "brown" dress set off by a *dramatic*-colored scarf creates a small but powerful "wow," allowing you to take center stage for your presentation or dazzle your prospective boss on that job interview.

You can then vary your "accent" pieces to create different effects. Substitute an *essence* note for the *dramatic* one, for example, and you instantly seem more open and emotionally available. Likewise, you might assume a calm, approachable air by wearing a casual "khaki" jersey wrap blouse with an *energy*-colored necklace. But switch that *energy*-colored necklace with a *romantic*-colored accessory and the whole outfit immediately becomes more romantic.

Sometimes, of course, you want the intensity of a *romantic*-colored dress or an *energy*-colored jacket. Other times, though, you want only small touches of these strong colors against a neutral backdrop. Either way, you don't need a dozen outfits, only three basics: formal "black" suit; relaxed "brown" dress or slacks-and-jacket combination; casual "khaki" shorts or capris. Combine these basics with just a few colorful items, and you can offer the world a dozen different aspects of yourself.

You can also switch *base* colors to vary the ways that your other colors appear. For example, if you're going to a cocktail reception, a *dramatic* robin's-egg-blue scoop-neck top is the perfect dressy "pop" when worn under a deep chocolate ("black") pantsuit in your formal *First Base* outfit. But when you wear the same *dramatic* top to a weekend clambake with your more casual vanilla ("khaki") capris—untucked, and with a skinny belt—it adds just enough zip to your relaxed *Third Base* look.

You get the idea: You can use your *three bases* as the foundation for many different looks. Because they can be varied with scarves, hats, and other accessories in one of your other colors, your *bases* are also excellent choices for your outerwear, as we'll see in Chapter 9. The key is to identify the *three base colors* that are perfect for you, rather than relying on a standard black, brown, or khaki that may not flatter your coloring at all.

When you scan the following lists, you may notice that some colors showing up here as "black," "brown," or "khaki" have already made their appearance as *essence, romantic, dramatic, energy,* or *tranquil* colors. That's not a mistake: That's the magic of your individual palette. The same eggplant that creates a *dramatic kaboom* for you appears on another woman as a quiet neutral; the olive drab that functions as your "brown" works on another woman as her *energy* or *tranquil* color. As you can see, color isn't absolute but rather a dynamic aspect of every woman's individual set of *true colors.* So get ready to celebrate your neutral colors, knowing that for some women, they may not be neutral at all.

FIND YOUR *THREE BASES*

1. Start by reviewing the "seeing" exercise on pages 24–29, just to get your eyes in shape.
2. Observe your eyes—if possible, in a magnifying mirror. Focus in on the ring around your iris. That

is your ***First Base,*** your version of black. Check out the nearby box for a list of possible ***First Base*** choices to help you identify this color.

3. Close your eyes for a moment to "cleanse" your vision before moving on to the next color. Now, using the same magnifying mirror and natural light, examine the underside of your hair. Look for the deepest tone—and be prepared to find colors you never thought were there. Check out the nearby box for a list of possible ***Second Base*** choices to help you identify your version of brown.

4. As before, close your eyes for a moment to "cleanse" your vision. Then, look at your natural highlights, the lightest part of your hair. Can you see taupe, rose beige, or perhaps wheat? Again, these tones may be unexpected—but discovering them can open your eyes to new possibilities in your palette. Look at the nearby box for a list of possible ***Third Base*** choices to help you identify your version of khaki.

HINT: If you're having trouble identifying colors, you might get some paint chips or even a box of crayons to match against your locks. Be open to finding unusual colors that you never thought of as belonging to "just brown" or "plain black" hair. You have a lot of choices for your ***bases,*** and the least obvious will often be the most interesting. So get creative and be willing to see past the obvious to something that is hard to identify— but incredibly rewarding to discover.

Covering Your Bases

If you color your hair, you will want to do this exercise using either your eyebrows or the underside of your hair—not the color or highlights you have artificially added. Nature designed your original hair color to flatter your skin and express your spirit, so try to recapture those colors as best you can when you choose your bases.

You may also be wondering how the aging process in general affects your palette. In fact, your *true colors* never fundamentally change—but they do tend to mellow a bit as you get older. The woman who once wore black, for example, might switch to a slightly softer version of off-black; the twenty-year-old whose "brown" was intense aubergine might become the forty-year-old whose "brown" is a somewhat less saturated aubergine. Your basic color vocabulary, however, remains the same.

Possible Candidates for Your *First Base, "Black"*

Grays and Blacks: Payne's gray, granite, charcoal, black, midnight, blue black

Blues: blueberry, dusty navy, navy, marine, Yale blue, deep cornflower, gray blue

Purples: dark hyacinth, dark plum, eggplant

Reds and Browns: bayberry, deep brick, dark auburn, Indian brown, molasses, chocolate, seal brown, coffee, dark walnut

Greens: olive, black green, dark emerald, British racing green, mountain pine

Possible Candidates for Your *Second Base, "Brown"*

Greens: olive drab, deep camouflage green, dark sage, dark anthracite green

Blues and Grays: slate gray, steel blue gray, deep admiral, cannon gray, gunmetal, flagstone, ash, mushroom

Browns: chocolate milk, bittersweet chocolate, milk chocolate, gingerbread, acorn, sepia, cognac, brandy, cordovan, russet

Purples: juniper berry, aubergine, deep plum, dark Concord grape, blue-violet shadow, old lavender

Possible Candidates for Your *Third Base, "Khaki"*

Grays and Greens: taupe, putty, khaki, frosted sage, olive gray, gray quartz, stone, silver, gray mist, dove gray, pearl

Off Whites and Beiges: alabaster, cream, vanilla, buff, ecru, wicker, wheat, sand, safari tan, honey beige, camel, champagne, almond, rose beige

Creating Your Authentic Style: Complete the exercise below and identify each of your Three Bases.

My *First Base* *(my version of BLACK)*:

_____

My *Second Base* *(my version of BROWN)*:

_____

My *Third Base* *(my version of KHAKI)*:

_____

BLACK IS BEAUTIFUL—EVEN WHEN
IT'S BLUEBERRY

If you have only one base-colored outfit in your wardrobe, I'd recommend going with your First Base, your version of "black." Black is the most formal neutral that you can wear, but it's also the most powerful.

We have lots of associations with black—associations that carry over even when your black is one of the other colors that serves as the *First Base* for your type. Black is a kind of uniform that allows us a bit of distance to hide behind. It connotes protocol, formality, and manners, creating a kind of uniform that focuses on the role rather than the individual. We Westerners, for example, wear black to funerals because we want the focus to be on our membership in the community that has come together to grieve, rather than distinguishing ourselves through our individual responses. So you can use your *First Base* to blend into the group, but you can also use it to provide a high-contrast backdrop to one of the other colors in your palette.

Black and its various versions also suggest a boundary or separation. Typically religious leaders, such as priests and nuns, wear dark colors—some version of black, dark blue, or dark brown—a *First Base* color that creates a little distance between them and their congregations and invites us to focus on their roles rather than their individual personalities.

You can buy a suit in your "black" to make a formal presentation, attend an important event, or simply add a touch of authority to your presence. You can also use this color for your shoes, briefcase, or purse to create a somewhat more formal look with your other outfits. Your formal *First Base* is a good color for a winter coat, hat, scarf, or gloves. You can use *First Base*-colored accessories—including jewelry, scarves, or a pashmina—to add more formality to other outfits. You might also use this color for the ink in your formal business pen and on your business cards.

Once you've bought your *First Base* formal outfit, you can dress it down, if you like, with other clothing items or accessories. You can become more approachable, for example, by adding an **essence**-colored blouse or an **energy**-colored scarf. **Romantic**-colored jewelry might make you feel and look sexier; **dramatic**-colored accents can add a touch of individualized power to your formal uniform.

Once you understand how to combine your *First Base* with other key colors, you can create a number of effective looks. If you're a Vivid Winter, for example, whose *Archetype* is the Earthy Philosopher and whose *First Base* "black" actually *is* black, you might wear a black dress and a black coat—and then line that coat in your *romantic* color, fire engine red. Imagine how brilliantly that red will pop against its neutral background! The red makes your wardrobe an event—vital, exciting. No matter which *Archetype* you are and which version of black you wear, you can also simply dress yourself in your *First Base* from head to toe, so that your own skin, eyes, and hair become the stars of the show, set off by your black backdrop.

However, not every type can employ every combination in the same way. For some types, a *First Base* plus a *romantic* blouse might offer a contrast that's simply too harsh. Most Autumns, for example, look better in blended colors. So if you're one of the six Autumn *Archetypes,* you might set off a *First Base* suit with a paisley blouse whose print includes *romantic, essence,* and *energy* colors, plus a few dots of your *First Base.* (You'll learn more about the contrast levels that are right for your *Archetype* when you read Chapter 6 and claim your *Archetype.*)

Get Down with Brown

If your First Base "black" is formal and uniform, your Second Base "brown" is more casual and individualizing. At work, you might wear your First Base to impress upon your team the importance of performing well. Your Second Base is a little mellower, a little more casual, but still somewhat formal, so you might wear it to be one of the team, maybe on a workday when you're not attending the Big Meeting. Your First Base could work for that important pitch to a new client or for a serious meeting with your top boss; your Second Base might work better for a day when you're more interested in supporting people than in impressing them.

Your **Second Base** is also a wonderful color for the summer, when things are more casual. In fact, at all but the most formal workplaces and for all but the most formal events, you won't be wearing your **First Base** nearly as often in the summer, making your **Second Base** a terrific alternative. Try it in more casual fabrics, too: Instead of the stiff, heavy fabrics that work well for your **First Base,** you can wear **Second Bases** in less dense materials such as suede, worsted wool, leather, or silk knit.

If your **First Base** color cries out for a suit, your **Second Base** probably wants to be trousers, a skirt, or a dress—something subtler and more casual. If your **First Base** goes with four-inch heels, your **Second Base** wants two-and-a-half- or three-inch heels. (And your **Third Base** calls for flats!) True, your **Second Base** "brown" creates more distance than your casual **Third Base** "khaki." But it's still warmer and less imposing than your **First Base** "black."

KICK BACK WITH YOUR KHAKI

You can rely on your informal "khaki" for casual clothes, like sundresses, shorts, and capris. This is a great color for weekend trousers, casual slacks, espadrilles, a windbreaker, a sun hat, and sunglasses. You can even buy a summer or even a winter suit in your "khaki" if you're going for a more informal look.

Your **Third Base** also calls for less formal fabrics: a cotton blouse, say, rather than charmeuse. To dress down your **First Base** or **Second Base** outfits, try some **Third Base** shoes, belts, or purses.

GETTING TO *FIRST BASE:*
BEING TRUE TO YOUR PALETTE

Let's get one myth out of the way. Contrary to popular notions, most people don't look great in black. It isn't necessarily slimming, nor is it flattering to anyone other than those Archetypes who actually can wear it: some Vital and Floral Springs; a few Jeweltone and Sunset Summers (who might wear a soft black); and some Classic, Soft, Dynamic, and Vivid Winters.

What everyone can do, though, is wear a *version* of black. Whatever your version of "black" turns out to be, your **First Base** should be flattering to your coloring so that you look attractive and like yourself. The right **First Base** won't distort your skin tone by making it look pale, green, or sallow. Nor should it be depressing. Instead, you'll find yourself quietly framed by a formal but supportive color that allows you a lot of different wardrobe choices.

My client Kati learned the power of finding her correct **First Base** in a particularly dramatic way. Before I started working with her, Kati was known as "the Lady in Black." A glamorous footwear executive, Kati simply lived in black. Whether at home or work, Kati wore black, black, and only black, the most beautiful, expensive, luxurious black there was. Whether the outfit was velvet, cashmere, silk, or suede, if it was black, high-priced, and in fabulous taste, Kati owned it. You could have staged a whole fashion show from her closet full of exquisite outfits.

The only problem was, Kati just didn't look good in black. Put her in a black outfit and she suddenly looked like a little girl playing dress-up. A good-looking woman in her early forties, Kati had a slim, curvy figure, but her gorgeously tailored black outfits made her look austere, even severe. The division she headed was based on cooperation and collaboration, but the image black-clad Kati projected was sharp and prickly, as though she were constantly muttering, "Don't get too close." That wasn't at all the message she wanted to convey—but her black wardrobe was speaking for her.

One day a woman who had become one of Kati's good friends at work said casually, "You know that photo you've got on your desk, the one of you at the picnic? You look amazing in that, by the way."

"Really?" Kati said, embarrassed. "That's such an old picture—I can't even believe I have it out."

"No," her friend insisted. "You've never looked prettier."

Significantly, in the picture, Kati wasn't wearing a single stitch of black. She wore a dusty fuchsia boat-necked blouse with long, pink-beige shorts. The colors brought out the glowing skin tones of her Playful Winter "Ballerina" *Archetype,* as well as her impish nature and her free-spirited, softer side.

Still, Kati didn't think the colors worked for her. "I'm a New Yorker," she told her friend. "I rely on my black. Besides, I'm not like you. I can't wear lots of different colors."

"I bet you could," the friend told her. "I didn't think I could, either, until I met David." Kati's friend had recently consulted with me and she was going through a kind of mini-renaissance, exploring all the beautiful colors we had discovered she could wear. "Now I see that black doesn't make me look my best," Kati's friend told her. "And why should I wear anything that doesn't make me look my best?"

Kati might never have taken her friend's advice to set up an appointment with me but for a chance remark of her husband's. The couple was preparing to go to a party and Kati was wondering what she was going to wear.

"Why are you wondering?" her husband asked her. "*I* know. You're going to wear black, aren't you? That's all you ever wear."

Kati started to feel as though she had taken on a whole alien identity. *I'm* not *the Lady in Black,* she said to herself. *I'm Kati.* She'd seen how her friend had blossomed as a person after she'd started to work with me, had seen how all the new colors in her friend's palette had brought out new colors in the friend's personality. She couldn't help wondering if she, too, could enjoy the same type of renaissance.

Reluctantly but with determination, Kati scheduled an appointment with me. The first thing she said was, "Please tell me that I don't have to give up my beautiful black things!"

"I don't want you to have to give up anything," I told her. "Let's just see which colors are in your palette."

When I suggested to Kati that black really *wasn't* her color, she grimaced. "I *have* to wear black, at least to work," she insisted. "I want people to take me seriously!"

I stood Kati in front of a mirror and held a black sweater up against her face. I showed her how black brought out every sharp line in her features, how unapproachable, harsh, and almost scary the color made her look.

Then I held up Kati's own "black," a deep, inky, midnight blue. The change was instant and dramatic. Her features softened, her skin took on the glowing ivory shade everyone had admired in her photograph, and her dark eyes seemed to grow larger and more luminous. Kati caught her breath.

"I think people will still take you seriously," I suggested. "But it will be the real you, not the Lady in Black."

Kati couldn't bring herself to get rid of her black clothes right away. She'd been using them as a kind of protection, and she wasn't sure what would happen if she gave those defenses up. But soon after our consultation, she and her husband were planning a European vacation and to prepare for it, the two of them went shopping. She caught sight of an inky blue dress in a store window and thought, *Well, I might as well try it on.*

As soon as she showed her husband what she looked like in the dress, he lit up. "You *have* to buy this dress!" he enthused. "I've never seen you look prettier. Please, please, *please,* get rid of your black dresses and buy this one!"

Kati looked at her husband in astonishment. "You've never said anything like that before," she said.

"Well," he said. "I never realized how harsh you looked in black until I saw the blue."

Kati had to accept that she'd been shielding herself in her beautiful black clothes. When she dressed herself in *her* "black," she felt lighter, which made her feel nervous but also freer. And when her husband said, "What else can we buy you in that color?" Kati knew it was time for a change.

The first time she wore her **First Base** dress to work, Kati felt like the belle of the ball. She got compliments from the guard at the front desk, the guy in the mailroom, the receptionist, her assistant. "Did you do something different to your hair?" one of them asked. "Have you lost weight?" queried another. No one knew what Kati had done, but everyone could see she looked better.

So Kati began to follow my other suggestions. She softened her silhouette, letting go of her shoulder pads, of the heavy buttons and buckles she'd armored herself in. She began to wear the clingy wrap dresses that befit a Playful Winter "Ballerina," creating a softer, more romantic line—authoritative, yes, but feminine, too. She began wearing different shoes—lighter, more playful, less spiky and harsh. Discovering her true **First Base** was Kati's first step in re-creating her wardrobe. More important, it was her first step in rediscovering herself.

THE POWER OF YOUR *TRUE COLORS*

Now that you've mastered your three bases, you've identified all of your true colors. You've also learned about the power of color to express different aspects of yourself and to create or support different moods.

With the understanding of the tones and shades that speak to your spirit, you've taken a giant leap forward in understanding your *authentic style*. But it's only the first step. Discovering your *Season* and claiming your *Archetype* will make the picture complete. So let's move on to the next two chapters for a look at how the individual colors in your palette add up to a distinctive whole.

Creating Your Authentic Style: Keep track of the discoveries you've made so far by filling out the following chart:

MY TRUE COLORS

My *Essence* Color *(my version of white, the skin tone that harmonizes the colors of my palm):* _____

My *Romantic* Color *(my version of red, the color that matches my face when I blush, my ears when they're cold, or a pinched fingertip):* _____

My *Dramatic* Color *(my version of blue, taken from the most dominant color of the veins in my wrist):* _____

My *Energy* Color *(taken from the darkest part of my iris):* _____

My *Tranquil* Color *(taken from the lightest part of my iris):* _____

My *First* Base *(my version of black, taken from the dark ring around my pupil):* _____

My *Second* Base *(my version of brown, taken from the darkest color of my hair or eyebrows):* _____

My *Third* Base *(my version of khaki, taken from the lightest color of my hair or eyebrows):* _____

5

it's only natural:

discovering your season

ever since the popular style book *Color Me Beautiful* was published, women have talked about which **Season** they are, Spring, Summer, Autumn, or Winter. Readers of that highly influential book have understood that their hair, eyes, and skin add up to a coherent palette, which they can use to distinguish between the colors that work for them and the colors that don't.

I think *Color Me Beautiful* has made an enormous contribution in helping women understand the power of **Season.** But I've also found that many women have misunderstood their **Season**—and as a result have chosen colors and looks that really aren't right for them. In my life as a designer and stylist, I've heard so many myths and misconceptions about color—all of which can be avoided if you just understand your **Season.**

For example, there's a prevalent myth that all redheads are Autumns. Not so. As we'll see in a moment, some Springs can be redheads, too. Then there are the racial and ethnic misunderstandings, such as that most African Americans and Asians are Winters and therefore look best in bold, high-contrast colors. On the contrary, you can't tell your *Season* simply by knowing your racial identification. First, especially in the United States, many of us are from mixed ethnic backgrounds. Second, even if you went to an isolated village in Senegal or a centuries-old hamlet in China, you would find people from all four *Seasons,* just like anywhere else in the world.

There are so many color myths out there: "Olive-skinned people shouldn't wear green because it brings out the green in their skin." "I'm fair, so I can't wear light colors because they'll wash me out." "My own coloring doesn't have a lot of contrast, so I need contrast or no one will notice me." No, no, no! Knowing your *Season* will help you choose the colors that flatter you and push you forward—the *true colors* based on your own unique coloring—which are the colors that bring out your personality and spirit.

I really came to understand the power of *Season* early in my career when I had two clients who happened to be identical twins. Clearly they looked about as much like each other as any two people could. Yet as I viewed them more closely, I began to see that even between these women whose genetic heritage was so similar, there were distinct differences in skin and eyes and hair, shades that contributed to making one of the women a Summer and the other a Winter. And guess what? The Summer was laid-back and calm and highly responsive to the emotional currents in a room, while the Winter was bold and forceful and tended to charge forward according to her own vision.

This early experience was a profound lesson in the ways that our *true colors* reflect our personality and spirit as well as our physical self. Understanding the power of *Season* has led me to perceive personality so accurately that some clients have even mistaken my talent for psychic ability!

The Elements of Your *Authentic Style*

Season: The set of colors and personality traits corresponding to one of the four seasons of the year; essential for understanding the colors, clothes, and objects that express your authentic self

---

Another powerful experience of **Season** came with a Midwestern college student I once worked with who was initially quite reluctant to reconsider her style. It was actually her mother who insisted that she give me a try, because a friend of the family's had recently had a consultation with me and had transformed her entire look as a result.

The daughter, Taylor, was a budding singer, with green eyes and soft red hair. She had somehow gotten the idea that all redheads were Autumns and that she had to wear deep burgundy, forest green, and dark, muddy browns. These, to her, were "autumnal" colors, and they included nothing that seemed bright, young, or playful.

"Look," she said bluntly when we first met. "I know my colors, and they're different from everybody else's. My coloring is just different, that's all."

In fact, Taylor was a perfect example of a Tawny Spring, whose **Archetype** is the Maverick. She was right to believe that she marched—or sang!—to the beat of a different drummer, but she didn't have the forceful personality of an Autumn, with its dry wit and sardonic humor. Instead, she was a bubbly, cheerful Spring, with a sassy, youthful quality that I could see was just waiting to be released from the dark greens and somber browns that Taylor typically wore.

"I mean, I get it," Taylor went on. "I know I'm different. I get that compared to everybody else, I'm a little bit . . . strange."

True, Taylor was the only redhead in her family. She was also the only family member interested in becoming a performer. And as a Maverick, she did have a quirky, one-of-a-kind quality as well. But she also had a huge reservoir of potential charm that simply wasn't being expressed, largely because the colors and clothes she always chose tended to isolate her. On Lizzie, whom you met in the Introduction, Autumn colors brought out a warmth and earthiness that drew people to her. But Autumn colors were wrong for Taylor, making her look harsh, sad, and somehow "off." She might not be like "everybody else"—but dressing as the wrong *Season* meant that she didn't look like herself, either.

I looked more closely at Taylor's delicate peach-colored skin and at the muddy green army jacket that was meant to set off her face. Again, I was struck by the contrast with Lizzie, whose skin had glowed with new warmth as soon as we put her in earth-toned shades. Wearing the very same colors made Taylor's skin look sallow and washed out. These colors brought her none of Lizzie's latent glamour; instead, they made her look sour and sulky.

I brought out the color chips that I always carry to a consultation and showed Taylor the hues I determined were her *true colors:* vivid teal, bright spearmint green, rosy coral. Like all Spring colors, they were bright and clear, evoking the sparkling sunlight of a bright spring day. I could see something in her respond to these *true colors,* but teenager-like, she wasn't quite ready to give in.

"I see you in colors like this," I told her. "With maybe a saucy beret or a novelty pin on your coat. Sassy, jaunty . . . *playful*. All your colors should be bright and clear—like a tempera painting. You've been dressing in oils—dark, muddy, rich. For some women, that would be a lovely look, but on you, it's too pensive and serious."

I could see that Taylor didn't want to agree with me, but she also couldn't help picking up the colors I had placed before her. I thought maybe a little more honesty was in order.

"As a performer, you should be drawing people to you," I told her. "And with your personality, you absolutely can. But is that happening now?"

"No," she admitted. "I'm just not that type of person. People like my singing—they tell me I have a great voice. But they don't exactly . . . I'm not exactly the kind of person who people seek out at a party or anything. But I'm okay with that! That's just not who I am."

"But it is," I insisted. "It's just that the way you're dressing is sending out a message: *Stay away, I'm hard and tough.* You could be saying, *Hey, come over here! We'll have a great time!* But in order to send out that message, you'll need to wear your ***true colors***— the colors that express your true self."

Like so many people her age, Taylor was reluctant to listen to what she thought of as "the voice of authority." But her responses to those ***true colors*** were so strong that she couldn't help giving them a try. "Just for a week," she warned me. "We'll see."

At the end of the week, Taylor was so excited that she couldn't stop talking. I heard about how she had just started dating a guy she had sort of liked but whom she had never quite clicked with. After she started wearing her ***true colors,*** though, he had actually sought her out after class, and a quick question about an assignment had somehow turned into a three-hour conversation, and then coffee, and then dinner. She'd gotten a warmer and more enthusiastic response at her weekend singing gig, and she thought she'd also performed at another level—

more magnetic, and more open. She did have one new problem: Suddenly so many people had started making excuses to talk to her on her way to class that, for the first time in her life, she was always late.

Since our first meeting, Taylor has gone on to longer relationships, more singing gigs, and a whole new comfort with her identity. Discovering the colors of her true **Season** was the key to expressing her authentic self and enjoying the life she'd been meant to live.

DISCOVERING YOUR *SEASON*

The Tony Award–winning actress Faith Prince was once a client of mine. I was honored to work with the performer who had starred in Broadway's *Guys and Dolls* and whom you may know from her role in Michael J. Fox's *Spin City*. When she saw the true colors I suggested for her, she beamed. "I don't know how you did it," she said in her trademark quirky voice, "but it's like a color map of my whole personality!"

If your *true colors* are your map, then knowing your **Season** is one way to quickly name your territory. The fact that **Seasons** are so important to expressing our true selves is part of our connection to nature, one profound way of knowing that we belong on this planet. But how, exactly, does knowing our **Season** help us to choose the colors, clothes, and objects that express our true selves?

Think of a winter landscape, perhaps the one in upstate New York, where I grew up. The sky is a pearly gray or maybe a luminous clear blue. The snow on the ground gleams diamond white out under the sun, but in the stark shadow of a farmhouse, its shade deepens into charcoal gray. The bare branches of the trees stand out sharply against the sky, while the crimson cardinal that perches for a moment on the nearest bough adds a brilliant note of contrast.

Now imagine a painting of that winter landscape—the pearly and charcoal grays, the clear blues, diamond whites, and crimson reds. The painting has been left out in the rain, perhaps, so that the objects—the trees, the bird, the farmhouse—become blurred. Nevertheless, the colors stay clear. You can recognize at a glance that distinctive winter palette—sharp, dramatic, high-contrast colors—and you can instantly see how it differs from, say, the pinks, purples, yellows, and greens that characterize spring.

The quiet aura of a country winter, with its sharply contrasting colors and its dramatic but hushed effect, should be echoed in the style choices of a Winter woman. As a general rule, Winters do best with clear, strong colors; sharp contrasts; and dramatic but quiet effects (less "Look at me!" than "Here I am"). When you picture the strong, simple lines of that winter landscape, you can see why a Winter woman might look too fussy in a frilly, ruffled blouse, why she might be too dramatic for a cute little pink scarf, and not "girly" enough for a floral-patterned skirt. Although, as we'll see, there are six different types of Winters, each with her own palette, fabric selection, and range of accessories, we can also see how every one of the Winter types is somehow at home in that striking landscape.

Now picture the lushness of a warm spring day, when the earth seems almost overpowered by a profusion of tender flowers, budding branches, and shooting spears of grass. Think of the bright greens and yellows as the sun sparkles off an apple tree, or the pinks and purples of a blooming clutch of hyacinths. The Spring woman thrives on floral patterns, sunny pastels, and playful accessories that capture all the newness and excitement of this season of beginnings. And although, again, there are six different types of spring—Vital Spring, Early Spring, Floral Spring, Buoyant Spring, Mischievous Spring, and Tawny Spring, each with its own ideal colors, clothes, and objects—all the Springs somehow embody the spirit of their *Season.*

The seasonal approach of *authentic style* involves far more than colors and fabrics. It's also about identifying energy that expresses itself in every way possible: through a person's skin, hair, and eye colors, certainly, but also through her actions, her tone of voice, her relationships, and her spirit. After twenty years of doing this work, I've gotten so I can identify a person's *Season* from only a few moments' conversation over the phone— and by the time you've mastered the principles of *authentic style,* you may be able to do the same!

The Sound of the Seasons: Identifying *Season* Through the Voice

Have I piqued your curiosity? Okay, I'll let you in on my trade secrets. After all, the whole point of this book is to empower you to recognize your own unique style, and how better to do that than to start recognizing the ways that *other* people express their styles?

Here's how I identify a new client's *Season* when the only contact I've had is a three-minute phone call:

- *Springs* are full of a kind of playful energy that always makes me think of blooming flowers and budding trees. Their voices have lots of range and fluctuation, capturing the "all over the place" feeling of an abundant spring meadow bursting with new life.
- *Summers* speak slowly, methodically, and with an even, mellow pace, much as they might stroll slowly along on a warm summer day. They choose their words carefully, too:

When the sun is blazing, you don't want to expend any extra energy!

- *Autumns* have sharp, clear voices that sound thoughtful and poised. If you listen to their crisp, somewhat brisk tones you can almost hear the crunch of twigs underfoot and sense the fragrance of dry leaves.

- *Winters* get right to the point. They speak with a bit more command than the other seasons, and you can feel in their tone the forcefulness of a high-contrast winter landscape, which almost seems to be saying, "Look at this, look at that, look at this."

Creating Your Authentic Style: Recall the Season you identified in Chapter 2. Read more about it in the section below. Be open to what your Season can tell you about the colors, clothes, and objects that are right for you.

1. Spring

Spring represents a reawakening of life and is the most buoyant of all the Seasons. The Spring type enjoys a fresh, light set of colors shot with sunlight: bright, dew-drenched, and radiant. The key to her true colors is clarity, as might be found in daisies or buttercups: Think of the French Impressionists, especially Renoir, Monet, and Manet.

For the Spring, every day is a new beginning. The sun is always shining, and everything seems possible. Accordingly the Spring is generally an optimistic type, excited by new ideas. For the Spring, variety is truly the spice of life; in fact, she's often quite happy to be distracted from her daily life if she can find something new and interesting in the distraction. No

matter what her actual age is, people think of the Spring type as
"youthful." She's typically fun loving and quite social, and she's
often the one thought of as sure to guarantee that everyone else
will have a good time, too.

Famous Spring personalities include Antonio Banderas, Kris-
tin Davis, Cameron Diaz, Cuba Gooding Jr., Tom Hanks, Goldie
Hawn, Sean Hayes, Nicole Kidman, Queen Latifah, Susan Lucci,
Isaac Mizrahi, Rachael Ray, Ryan Seacrest, Will Smith, Reese
Witherspoon, and Renée Zellweger.

2. Summer

Summer coloring features luxurious tones suggesting the
expansive, relaxed feeling of life in warm climates where the
sun is always shining. The sun bakes the Summer colors into
colors that are hazier, more shaded, and chalkier than those of
the Spring, often touched with a morning mist, or softened and
blended in the evening dews. Think of the hazy, shaded colors found in the paintings of Gainsborough and Romney, and
you'll understand the beauty of the Summer's true colors.

The Summer personality tends to go with the flow, living
her life in an even, mellow rhythm. Of course, sometimes she
gets stressed like everybody else, but her natural tempo is more
serene. She tends to be a good diplomat who knows that there
are always two sides to every story—at least!—and that every
point of view has its merits. Honest and detail-oriented—you
can't hide anything under that Summer sun!—she is also nurturing and warm, and she understands the importance of rest
and reflection better than any of the other Seasons. If you think
of the stillness and magical quality of a summer landscape, you'll
understand why true beauty often stops the Summer type in

her tracks. That sense of wonder is Summer's gift, and at her best, she knows how to make the most of it.

Well-known Summer personalities include Alec Baldwin, Halle Berry, Ed Burns, Tom Cruise, Giada De Laurentis, Michael Douglas, Jennifer Garner, William Hurt, Beyoncé Knowles, Brad Pitt, Diane Sawyer, Leelee Sobieski, Meryl Streep, Uma Thurman, Meredith Vieira, and Denzel Washington.

3. Autumn

The true colors of Autumn are forceful with a burnished cast: dry, spicy, smoky, and blazing, with brilliant and tawny tones. The rich mellow harvest, when the earth turns back into itself and the wind whips the trees, suggests the qualities of the Autumn's true colors, as do the paintings of Rembrandt and Toulouse-Lautrec.

The Autumn personality is typically hard-working and diligent, taking pride in her accomplishments. This mind-over-matter type is often the last warrior standing, unwilling ever to accept defeat. Great with deadlines, she often has to force herself to relax and recharge. Autumns are blessed with a dry wit, a sardonic sense of humor, and the gift of laughing at themselves. They have a natural sense of authority, which they may use either to take charge or to work quietly behind the scenes. Either way, you'll recognize the earthy power of an Autumn.

Famous Autumn personalities include Lauren Bacall, Angela Bassett, Joy Behar, Hillary Rodham Clinton, Jodie Foster, Bill Maher, Angelina Jolie, Patti LuPone, Madonna, Debra Messing, Julianne Moore, Sarah Jessica Parker, Kiefer and Donald Sutherland, Emma Thompson, Oprah Winfrey, Kate Winslet, and Hilary Swank.

4. Winter

Winter is the season of contrast. Still, silent, cool, and brilliant, like icicles, moonlight, and silver, Winter causes the eye to stop and the spirit to rest. Winter's true colors, as well as their combinations, carry through this theme: Think of poinsettias flaming against snow. Of course, not every winter contrast is as strong as black against white—for some Winters, charcoal against oyster is more like it—but the idea of contrast is still central. Picture the drawings of Da Vinci and the paintings of El Greco, and you'll understand the true colors of a Winter woman.

Solitude is precious to most Winters as a time to recharge, just as the earth uses the winter season to restore itself and prepare for a new season of life and growth. Accordingly Winters tend to avoid chaos and situations likely to produce chaos, though they are also very good at establishing order. A good judge of character, the Winter is a loyal friend with a keen analytical mind, though she has to watch out for a tendency to see the world in black and white, with very few shades of gray. Her sense of integrity is so deep and strong, however, that she's often the one to whom others turn for a sense of right and wrong.

Well-known Winter personalities include Orlando Bloom, Anderson Cooper, Penélope Cruz, Johnny Depp, Teri Hatcher, Anne Hathaway, Keira Knightly, Sandra Oh, Sidney Poitier, Christina Ricci, Winona Ryder, David Strathairn, Rachel Weisz, and Catherine Zeta-Jones.

"I can't believe she wore *that!* . . ."

Have you ever watched an awards ceremony or a red-carpet feature on TV and marveled at how bad your favorite actresses looked when they stepped out of the silver screen? I guarantee that most of the time what you're seeing is the effects of women dressing out of their *Season.* Even if you're movie-star gorgeous, dressing like an Autumn when you're really a Spring—or vice versa—will do terrible things to your skin, eyes, hair, and spirit, while wearing your *true colors* will immediately boost both your beauty and your personal charm.

Next time you watch an awards show, notice who looks good in her outfit and who doesn't. Then see if you can identify whether she's wearing the colors that are right for her. Unfortunately many stars and their stylists are dazzled by "the latest thing" or by the beauty of a dress in and of itself, without understanding how the dress interacts with the *Season* of the woman wearing it. What I've found is that when you're in tune with your *Season,* you're at home in the world; but when you're not, you're not—even if you're one of the world's most beautiful women.

FROM SEASON TO ARCHETYPE

Discovering your *Season* is an important step—but before you can truly fulfill your *authentic style,* you have one more step to go. Now it's time to claim your *Archetype,* which you'll learn how to do in the next chapter.

6

from prom queen to sensuous backpacker:

claiming your archetype

when I first studied color and style in 1989, the four seasons approach had just come into vogue. Clients who had read one of the many books and articles drawing on that system would frequently announce happily, "I'm a Spring!" or inform me gravely that they were a Winter.

I loved the four seasons approach, but to me, it was incomplete. How could you confuse the rusty brick and off white of an Antique Winter with the bright blue red and alabaster of a Classic Winter, or mistake the deep teals and burgundies of a Renaissance Summer for the sky blues and gentle violets of an Iridescent Summer? Along with every color theorist I knew, I could see significant variations within each season, subtypes whose *true colors* differed from one another, often quite dramatically.

For example, both the Vital Spring and the Tawny Spring partake of the youthful, vigorous, playful energies of their signature season. But a Vital Spring's *Archetype* is the Prom Queen. She's born to be the center of attention, the popular girl, the one who pulls a party together, and her palette glistens like a burgeoning flowerbed, with its clear pink, Kelly green, and blueberry.

Tawny Spring, on the other hand, is a Maverick, a quirky self-starter who's usually listening to the beat of her own distant drummer. She may not even show up at the prom, and if she does, she may bring that drummer with her and dance to an entirely different rhythm than everybody else! Her palette expresses another side of spring, with its mossy greens and woodsy browns. Both are Springs—but their *Archetypes* help define the precise styles that are right for them.

I've found that helping my clients claim their *Archetypes* is an important part of my work as a stylist. Identifying your *true colors* is important—but taking it one step further and seeing those colors as part of a coherent personal type really empowers you to understand your *authentic style* and to become even more clear and focused about choosing the colors, clothes, and objects that express your authentic self. Although fashions change and our tastes may change, too, over the years, our *Archetype* never changes. The Prom Queen at age twenty may dress differently than the Prom Queen at thirty, fifty, or seventy, but she's still working with the same basic palette and she's still expressing her "life of the party" spirit.

The Elements of Your *Authentic* Style

Archetype: The set of colors, style choices, and personality traits corresponding to one of the six subtypes of a *Season;* essential for understanding the colors, clothes, and objects that express your authentic self

Of course, as with all aspects of your ***authentic style,*** claiming your ***Archetype*** should be not an end, but a beginning. Once you understand this aspect of your personal style, you can go on to make it even *more* personal, putting your own unique twist on how you choose that ideal charm bracelet or that perfect clingy sweater or that amazing little jacket. Claiming your ***Archetype*** is only the first step in developing your own ***authentic style***—but it's a very important step, giving you a vision of the colors, clothes, and objects that are likely to work for you, and helping you to understand why. It can sometimes feel a little hard to claim the beauty of an ***Archetype*** for yourself, but go ahead. Do it. Let yourself be a Classic Beauty or a Prom Queen. You have it in you. I promise.

So let's get started! As I've found with my clients, claiming your ***Archetype*** may just be the most exciting step of all!

Creating Your Authentic Style: Recall the Season you identified in Chapter 2. Find it in the section below. (Spring, pages 94–109; Summer, pages 109–125; Autumn, pages 126–142; Winter, pages 142–158.) Read all six Archetypes for your Season. Then claim the Archetype that seems right for you.

HINT: For extra fun, see if you can identify ***Archetypes*** for your friends and coworkers, too! Then start to look at their wardrobes in terms of their ***Archetype***. Once you understand other people's ***authentic style,*** you're likely to discover new insights and ideas about your own.

WHAT'S YOUR *AUTHENTIC STYLE*?:
UNDERSTANDING THE TWENTY-FOUR ARCHETYPES

Spring

1. Vital Spring

Archetype:
The Prom Queen.

Celebrities:
Kristin Davis, Eva Longoria, Susan Lucci, Rachael Ray.

Motto:
"That sounds like fun!"

Secret Superpower:
Charm, charm, and more charm. The world's hostess! Invite a
Vital Spring to your dinner party and you guarantee a great
evening for all: She will keep the crowd entertained while you
are slaving in the kitchen.

Kryptonite:
When it's no longer fun, she often doesn't want to play
anymore.

Nature Image:
Zinnias, French parrot tulips, Gerbera daisies, pompoms.

Artists:
Mondrian and Matisse for the high-contrast primary colors.

Charming Contrasts:
High-contrast outfits and accessories will always make the
Prom Queen look terrific—a red scarf to set off a black
coat, or white polka dots on a blueberry-colored umbrella.

Her look is even better in "surprise" contrast that leads you to expect the unexpected. She might consider a vivid *dramatic*-colored coat lining, or a *First Base* outfit and shoes punctuated with a *romantic*-colored handbag, or an *energy*-colored enamel charm on her bracelet.

Fabulous Fabrics:

The fabrics are crisp and include cotton piqué, cotton sateen, faille, bouclé, patent leather, and satin.

Signature Scent:

Citrus: It's brisk, bold, and does not linger.

Must-Haves:

The Prom Queen favors a Chanel-inspired bouclé jacket (she may even splurge for a real one!), nautically styled gabardine pants, a slim pegged skirt, a button-front blouse with pearl buttons, and a crisp cotton belted shift dress. Her silhouette is clean in line and efficient with a dash of costume elements thrown into the mix. Though her look is crisp and refined, all of her favorite pieces are reminiscent of vintage styles and possess an air of "I get things done."

When it comes to styles, she's most at home in a 1950s look: crisp, clean, with a little bit of movement. Think swing coats and swirly skirts, perhaps contrasted with a structured purse. Frequently sought-after in social situations, Vital Springs also do well wearing conversation pieces: a charm bracelet, for example, or a dark vintage-inspired coat with a bright high-contrast lining.

Must-Avoids:

The Vital Spring should avoid burnished colors or ensembles made up of muted, blended colors and fabrics. She's always best in high contrast with a touch of novelty. And she should pass on the cowboy boots and anything oversized. Cowboy boots have too many varied lines in them and actually are more of a design suitable for Autumns. The woman who wears them has a kind of I-roll-up-my-sleeves-and-shoot-pool-with-the-boys quality. This does not describe the Prom Queen, though she will be game for pool—but sporting a pair of capris, a crisp blouse, and a small neck scarf. She always keeps her playful femininity, no matter what she's doing. As for oversized items, the crisp pert lines that favor this type illustrate her efficient I-get-things-done manner, whereas oversized connotes an I'll-get-to-it-but-right-now-I'm-just-hangin' mentality.

Personality and Spirit:

There's a good reason why Vital Springs have that Prom Queen image—they're the most charming, outgoing, and friendly of the Archetypes. They're the kind of people who become best friends with everyone in the room five minutes after they walk in, and others often develop crushes on them. That's no surprise: They radiate the kind of energy and magnetism that draws people in, and no matter what the situation, they tend to lead with a smile. With her independent spirit, the Prom Queen functions best when given a lot of leeway, but don't worry—she'll charm her boss and colleagues into an arrangement that works well for everybody.

2. Early Spring

Archetype:

The Playful Princess.

Celebrities:
Angela Lansbury, Gwyneth Paltrow, Chloë Sevigny, Naomi
Watts.

Motto:
"How amusing!"

Secret Superpower:
An instinct for what's most important. Count on the Early
Spring to always get to the heart of the matter.

Kryptonite:
Not being appreciated—that causes the Early Spring to droop
like a wilted flower.

Nature Image:
Crocuses poking their tips up through the snow, gladiolus, iris.

Artists:
Monet and the other Impressionists, whose cool saturated
pastels are perfect for Early Springs.

Charming Contrasts:
For the Playful Princess, light and easy low-contrast is best.
As this palette is very gentle, I would suggest never wearing
more than two groups of her colors together at the same time.
For example, a **Third Base** suit could be paired with a pastel
romantic blouse, as well as jewelry, shoes, and a scarf that pick
up these tones, perhaps in different values.

The Early Spring should use pattern in the way it is seen
in Monet's *The Water Lilies:* small, delicate brush strokes, each
dollop of paint slightly blended into the one beside it, giving
the overall impression of a landscape seen through a train
window on a rainy day. Confetti patterns also work well for

her. No eye-popping high-contrast patterns, please—they just don't suit her gentle palette.

Fabulous Fabrics:
Cashmere, organza, suede, and especially, crisp cottons. No other type looks as good in a crisp winter-white cotton blouse.

Signature Scents:
Gentle, flowery, soft, and powdery—but with a slight kick, such as jasmine.

Must-Haves:
The Playful Princess favors a simple polished-cotton pastel Agent 99 trench coat, Hollywood waisted pants, a slim waistband-less skirt, a crisp cotton blouse worn with a thin belt over it, and an updated version of the shirtdress with the collar popped up. The demure, playful Early Spring can pull off a beret or even a cloche hat, something sleek and close to the head. She's the type for whom blouses with bows were invented, and for a little light-handed playfulness, try chinos embroidered with a novelty design—but no belt loops, and with a back zipper, please!

Her wardrobe suggests a cool, sleek, playful elegance, someone sweet and flowery—but with a kick. While she can wear clothing derived from masculine dress such as trousers, all her garments need to be curved and adapted to her feminine shape. Adding a slight dose of irony doesn't hurt, either.

Must-Avoids:
Denim. Although the Early Spring looks great in slim trousers with no waistband, she has a terrible time finding the right pair of blue jeans—because they don't suit her! She needs to avoid

anything even remotely masculine. Hence, our Early Spring should pass on the men's-style trench with epaulets and patch pockets as well as on popping printed patterns. The original version of this trench is too masculine and too literal; and high contrast prints are too harsh for her delicate coloring.

Personality and Spirit:

Early Springs are ladylike, yes, and somewhat proper, and perhaps even demure, but they're also blessed with a lively curiosity and a strong sense of fun. There's an appealing coolness to the Early Spring, the slight formality that often marks someone with beautiful manners and that air of "to the manner born," but there's also a playful, inquisitive nature lurking just below the surface. Count on the Early Spring to show up at that all-important job interview, impeccable in a dove-gray suit and a pearly white blouse—and then to tell a silly joke that surprises the interviewer into delighted laughter. A good girl she may be—but she's got her share of pluck.

3. Floral Spring

Archetype:

The Wholesome Flirt.

Celebrities:

Doris Day, Barbara Walters, Reese Witherspoon, Renée Zellweger.

Motto:

"Live for today."

Secret Superpower:

Making the most of every moment.

Kryptonite:
Realizing that she is making a mistake in the middle of making it and then becoming self-conscious.

Nature Image:
Daffodils, hyacinth, and tulips.

Artist:
Fragonard.

Charming Contrasts:
Wholesome Flirts do best with crisp contrast. Offering relief from head-to-toe color is good, such as a crisp blouse in her shade of white peering out from under an *energy*-colored suit accessorized with a pearl necklace. In such an outfit, the white doesn't punctuate, but rather gives the eye a break from all of that *energy* color and creates a halo around the wearer's face, enabling the Floral Spring to win the attention that she loves.

Fabulous Fabrics:
Though she is feminine, the Floral Spring's fabrics need to stay crisp. Camel's hair, gabardine, eyelet, and organdy are best.

Signature Scents:
Sweet and floral. Even when she's all grown up, she might try a strawberry-scented lip balm.

Must-Haves:
The Floral Spring favors a brightly colored peacoat, slim trousers with side slits at the ankle, an A-line skirt, a cute sweater set, and a shift dress covered in pastel paillettes. These are the garments that flatter the Wholesome Flirt, with her ultra-feminine, always flirty nature. She enjoys incorporating costume-y elements into her wardrobe—such as a bow-shaped clutch or sandals decorated with a bumblebee buckle—but all

her choices need to be frothy and flirtatious, never influenced by anything practical unless it's a reinvention of something practical, such as the revamping of a sailor's peacoat in a vivid color with theatrically sized buttons.

Must-Avoids:
Austere or severely styled clothing. This woman must always wear clothing which complements her carefree, flirty, feminine nature. Hence, the Wholesome Flirt should pass on camouflage cargo pants and one-shoulder gowns—the pants are too serious and the one-shoulder gown, too asymmetrical, which makes her look imbalanced and, oddly, staid.

Personality and Spirit:
Like the coquettish beauty batting her baby blues at two men in Fragonard's *The Swing,* this Archetype embodies the words *feminine* and *flirtatious.* The Floral Spring sometimes seems like an enchanted creature who lived in a garden all her life and somehow decided to venture out into the world of more ordinary mortals. Like many of their Spring sisters, the Floral Springs are charming beyond belief, but their charm is always genuine. If you feel good in their presence, it's because they really do see the best in everything and everyone, including you, and they have a gift for making you believe in the magic that seems all too apparent to them. That may be why they're the most flirtatious of the Archetypes: If life is a garden, why not sample every flower?

4. Buoyant Spring

Archetype:
The Life of the Party.

Celebrities:
Cameron Diaz, Goldie Hawn, Queen Latifah, Amy Poehler.

Motto:
"How interesting!"

Secret Superpower:
Enthusiasm. Everything fascinates her.

Kryptonite:
Sometimes that all-encompassing enthusiasm can become just a little . . . well, scattered.

Nature Image:
Sunflowers, buttercups, daisies, button poms, cosmos, tuberoses, foxglove.

Artist:
Matisse, for the high-contrast use of color.

Charming Contrasts:
The Life of the Party needs a pattern somewhere in her outfit or accessories in order to tie together the entire look. She can unify a *romantic*-colored shirt and ***Third Base*** capris with plaid sandals that feature both of those colors. As an extra plus, those sandals are also a wonderful conversation-starter!

Fabulous Fabrics:
Poplin, organza, embroidered cotton, linen, stretch satin.

Signature Scents:
Sporty, invigorating, perhaps with a hint of eucalyptus. A splash rather than a cologne works better, as it is lighter and less serious.

Must-Haves:

A blazer cut to the high hip with an accentuated waist is
the perfect garment for the Life of the Party, as are capris, a
turtleneck with short puffed sleeves, and a metallic brocade
shift dress adorned with feathers at the hem. Savoring life to
the fullest is what she's all about, and she needs her wardrobe
to reflect this.

Must-Avoids:

Hyperformality—and not only in clothing. The Buoyant
Spring also has the urge to do something zany to break the
tension at a party that is too stuffy. The results may be, um,
problematic—or they could be delightful. The Buoyant Spring
needs to pass on the chiffon caftan and motorcycle-inspired
looks. The caftan would make her seem like a dowager, and no
matter what her real age, the Buoyant Spring is always young
at heart. Also, the caftan feels a bit too grand for her. At heart
the Buoyant Spring is the girl who genuinely enjoys kicking
off her shoes at the end of the day. Any article of clothing that
conveys an aura of queenly grandness feels too serious for
this fun-loving type, especially since it limits so severely the
number of fashion choices she can make—no belt, no skirt, no
scarf, just a pair of sandals and some jewels. As for motorcycle-
inspired ensembles, while the Life of the Party is fun and game
for most anything, a boots-and-leather look hardens her I-
love-being-a-girl silhouette and limits her opportunity for the
adornment of her favorite fashion element: herself!

Personality and Spirit:

Playful, sporty, and energetic, the Buoyant Spring is brimming
over with high spirits and good cheer. Her buoyant energy
lends itself more to shorts or capris than to a full-length

evening gown, though when she does put on that fancy dress, you may be surprised to realize how pretty she is. The Buoyant Spring is always a marvelous cheerleader. She knows how to draw other people out, encouraging them to express their most cherished ideas—and then she knows how to make those ideas sound brilliant.

5. Mischievous Spring

Archetype:
The Pixie.

Celebrities:
Tyra Banks, Bernadette Peters, Rosie Perez, Rihanna, Julia Roberts.

Motto:
"Everything I really want eventually comes to me."

Secret Superpower:
Huge confidence in herself.

Kryptonite:
Expects everyone to come to her, which means sometimes she can be a bit selfish—perhaps even more than a bit.

Nature Image:
Lily pad, buttercup, bluebells.

Artists:
Landscape artists who paint the French countryside.

Charming Contrasts:
Gentle contrast is best for our Pixie, but she can handle more contrast in a single outfit than most of the other Springs can

manage. For the weekend, she might look for a longish belted tweed coat in her *energy* color over a short skirt and tights in her *Third Base* color, accented by a metallic and *energy*-colored purse, metallic earrings, and a few favorite odd mismatched bracelets.

Fabulous Fabrics:
Lightly textured knits, brushed cotton, embossed suede, organza, crisp cotton, piqué.

Signature Scents:
Narcissus, hyacinth.

Must-Haves:
A softly tailored short anorak, short-sleeved knit sweater with self-belt and collar, slim stretch cigarette pants, miniskirt with pleated hem, bouclé knit hooded cardigan, and halter-style printed maxidress create the pixieish look of the Mischievous Spring. Our Pixie always needs the element of surprise incorporated into her mischievous style or else she looks out of place. A well-fitting dress with very simple lines is fine for New Year's Eve, but she would need a marabou shrug or a feathered headband in order to keep the outfit from seeming too stuffy.

Must-Avoids:
Big ruffles at her cuffs, which just look silly waving all over the place. The Mischievous Spring should also avoid wide-legged trousers, full-skirted gowns, and layered dresses, all of which tend to make her look like a little girl playing dress-up or like a delicate pixie drowning in waves of fabric. She should also avoid a too-polished head-to-toe look as well as any garment or accessory that proclaims, "I am serious."

Personality and Spirit:
When I think of the Mischievous Spring, I think of the sound of jingle bells: This pixieish creature evokes everything that is frolicsome and fun, and like all Springs, the Mischievous Spring is charm personified. She often works quite hard, but unless you pay close attention, you may not realize it: She may create the impression that a battery of elves magically completed her assignments overnight. The Mischievous Spring sometimes seems like the ultimate free spirit, but somehow, she always meets her deadlines, shows up on time, and comes through like a trouper. It's just that her process for getting there might drive more organized types insane. She's the kind of woman who can show up at a party looking stunning even though she just bought the dress that morning and then couldn't find the right lipstick and had to borrow a neighbor's. No matter how she got there, she always looks fantastic—and there she is, ready to share her mischievous sense of fun with everyone else at the party.

6. Tawny Spring

Archetype:
The Maverick.

Celebrities:
Amy Adams, Carol Burnett, Ginger Rogers.

Motto:
"I am my own trendsetter."

Secret Superpower:
Being just a little bit ahead of the curve and bringing other people along with her.

Kryptonite:
Sometimes she just can't get past that one niggling detail—the fly in the ointment, the one thing that tarnishes the whole. Frustration with something relatively minor can sometimes spoil the whole thing for her.

Nature Image:
Poppies, green euphorbia, yarrow, pear blossom, ranunculus.

Artists:
Renoir, Rousseau.

Charming Contrasts:
As befits a Maverick, the Tawny Spring puts together diverse elements in a way that she couldn't possibly explain to anyone else. Clearly this type will also put together her contrast levels in precisely the way that she wants to! Her "find" of a vintage 1960s *tranquil*-colored blouse is made fresh and interesting when worn over a *Second Base* turtleneck and paired with skinny-fit *Second Base* trousers. Mavericks take warning: Never wear shades of the same color, as the exchange of energy between the similar shades is not dynamic enough, creating a muddy effect.

Fabulous Fabrics:
Pony, light popcorn tweeds, embossed leather, knit fabrics.

Signature Scents:
She will probably favor a mixture of citrus and spice. She is eclectic, so she will probably have several small bottles of different scents. None of them will be floral or powdery.

Must-Haves:
Our Maverick favors an updated military-styled jacket, boot-cut trousers, a miniskirt worn with tights, a vintage 1960s

blouse, and a button-front knit sweater dress with contrasting collar and cuffs worn over a tank. After all, her motto is "I am my own trendsetter," and what better outfits to choose than those that allow her a fertile field for her creative vision. The Maverick is eclectic in her style and is best in slightly theatrical pieces. She is the type that can easily wear a feathered cloche, fingerless gloves, or a plaid capelet—and even better if they are all worn at the same time! If her outfit looks like a costume from the forest scene in Shakespeare's *As You Like It,* the one in which shepherds and shepherdesses frolic, she will love it. She will find it difficult to pass a vintage clothing store without stopping in.

Must-Avoids:

Clothing that is uniform or "matched," such as a matching blazer and skirt. This type should never own a suit; she needs to make a statement by putting together diverse pieces in unexpected ways. She should also pass on the long flowing skirts and any clothing influenced by minimalism. She is too "ready for action" and her energy is too high for the languid I-go-with-the-flow quality of drapey soft chiffon, which in any case suggests genteel beauty, rather than the Tawny Spring's air of sprightly fun. Finally, no minimalism for the Maverick: When you strip this energetic creature down to monochromatic minimalism, she will feel and act as though she is at a wake.

Personality and Spirit:

Quirkiest of all the Spring Archetypes, the Tawny Spring is nearly impossible to pin down. She has a habit of zigzagging from one activity to another. Yet she's reliable and trustworthy, and there's a method to her madness. The Tawny Spring views the world not through rose-colored glasses, exactly, but let's say through teal-colored ones: a unique, distinctive perspective that is all her own, and that to everyone else seems slightly askew. When everyone else sees the forest, she notices that one little branch over in the corner, where a rare tropical species has just built its nest. Then she wonders why no one else can see that little sliver of teal-colored feather that tipped her off—it seems blatantly obvious to her!

Summer

1. Classic Summer

Archetype:
The Classic Beauty.

Celebrities:
Katherine Heigl, Scarlett Johansson, Grace Kelly, Beyoncé Knowles, Diane Sawyer, Charlize Theron.

Motto:
"Harmony above all."

Secret Superpower:
All she has to do is show up. You know how some people simply have to walk through the door to brighten up a room? That's the hallmark of a Classic Summer.

Kryptonite:
Things being out of harmony throws this woman for a loop.

Nature Image:
Peony, cabbage rose.

Artists:
Thomas Gainsborough, John Singer Sargent.

Charming Contrasts:
Gentle contrast is best for the Classic Beauty, with values of
colors worn in similar values from head to toe. She should go
for high contrast only in small amounts, such as the piping
on her jacket or perhaps in her jewelry, such as a sapphire and
white-gold pendant contrasting with a *First Base* wrap dress.
She should avoid high contrasts in larger garments, such as
romantic-colored pants with a *Second Base* jacket, because on
her, the look will seem restless and imbalanced.

Fabulous Fabrics:
Cashmere, camel's hair, sueded silk, silk knit, cotton organdy.

Signature Scents:
This type often feels overwhelmed by perfume and will
frequently wear it only in an after-bath powder. The scent may
contain the essence of lavender.

Must-Haves:
The Classic Summer's wardrobe should include an open-styled
jacket without buttons, a cowl-neck sweater, straight trousers
with a comfortable waistband, a gabardine fishtail skirt, a long
cashmere wrap sweater closed with a shell-shaped pin, and a
wrap-style halter dress. These are the languid, elegant garments
that set off this Classic Beauty's classic beauty. This cool,
put-together, and ultra-feminine woman would look right at
home in the garments of ancient Greece—or in their modern
equivalents: a wrap dress, a clingy sweater, a draped skirt. Think
of a beautiful piece of fabric draped and folded to create the
most effortless, timeless, and absolutely beautiful effect, and
you'll know how to dress the Classic Summer.

Must-Avoids:

The Classic Beauty should pass on animal prints and any garment featuring grommets. Her classic style goes best with simple, clean, uncomplicated lines and beautiful fabrics, and her comfort zone is fixed firmly in the realm of the well-cut and high-quality—traits that ill accord with the exoticism of animal prints. Likewise, grommets—and anything else reminiscent of industrial design—are too hard for this type, who prefers a tactile, caressable quality to anything sleek, rough, or industrial. Besides, industrial elements are just too functional for the Classic Beauty, who is practical but who favors beauty over function.

Personality and Spirit:

The Classic Summer is all about appropriateness and protocol, not because she's rigid or old-fashioned, but because she's so devoted to harmony. She will always appear charming in public even to her archenemy. She will, however, deafen her date's ears on the ride home, explaining why she dislikes her nemesis so very much. She is also a bit of a dreamy adventuress: She may read an article about an exotic place and several weeks later might book a trip there because she found the description so appealing. The Classic Beauty has high expectations, of others as well as of herself. She can often be quite demanding, but that's only because she herself is prepared to give so much. Loving, devoted, and loyal to a fault, she'll defend you to the death once she's decided that you're on her "list," and you'll never know a better friend or a more steadfast partner.

2. Jeweltone Summer

Archetype:
The Glamorous Career Girl.

Celebrities:
Tina Fey, Andie MacDowell, Katharine McPhee, Jaclyn Smith.

Motto:
"I'll take care of that."

Secret Superpower:
She's always right. Really. Don't fight it. She is.

Kryptonite:
She has a very hard time delegating. And why not? When you're always right, it's hard to let go and let other people potentially make mistakes.

Nature Image:
Violet, anemone, hyacinth, American Beauty rose.

Artist:
Ingres.

Charming Contrasts:
Of all the Summer types, our Glamorous Career Girl wears the outfits with the most contrast, but she must make sure to pull the whole look together with an accessory so her ensemble doesn't seem like a cubist piece of art. A *dramatic*-colored knit dress worn with a **Second Base** coat and a long necklace that has elements of both colors is beautiful on her.

Fabulous Fabrics:
Cashmere knit, satin-faced wool, wool jersey, cotton poplin.

Signature Scents:
Rose, geranium.

Must-Haves:
The Glamorous Career Girl would look terrific in a velvet single-breasted blazer. She should run out and get some fit-and-flare jeans in her *First Base* color, as well as a 1940s-inspired chiffon skirt, a portrait-collar sweater, and a ribbed-knit wrap dress with a self-belt. Everything about her is brisk and glamorous, often with a forties flair.

Must-Avoids:
While structure is important to this type, it is important that her clothing not become overly rigid. Her figure needs to dictate her clothing, and her feminine curve and graceful gait need to be accentuated. She does not do well in a situation where she is supposed to take on the persona of a man, as this type is ultrafeminine—but strong. The Jeweltone Summer should definitely pass on miniskirts and geometric patterns. Miniskirts create a harsh horizontal and make her appear short waisted even if she is not. Most patterns do not work for her, especially geometric ones, because she is truly best in vivid blocks of color. Her coloring has such a warm inviting glow that simply having large washes of flattering color next to her completes her portrait. Geometric patterns, even when they're comprised of her colors, compete for attention with her lushness and create lines of energy that are too frenetic for her spirit.

Personality and Spirit:
You know that 1940s movie character, the Glamorous Career Girl? That feminine but never frou-frou brunette in the jersey wrap dress with the big earrings, the one who seems

supercompetent, charming, and dryly witty, all at the same time? Well, that's our Jeweltone Summer. You can just see her striding through the office, thoroughly in charge, but always warm and comradely. Only she could mix the friendly greeting, "Did you win the tournament on Saturday?" with the crisp command, "Have that press release on my desk by two." She's a great manager, but somehow she manages never to lose her feminine aura. This is the kind of woman who can wear soap instead of cologne and somehow make it seem sexy. She's the kind of woman you can count on to drop everything to comfort you when your latest boyfriend dumped you—but somehow she'll be back in the office at two in the morning, finishing her reports on time. She's also the kind of woman who's known and loved by everyone in her neighborhood— the clerk at the corner grocery, the mail carrier, the gas station attendant—all of whom appreciate her warmth, friendliness, and open-heartedness.

3. Sunset Summer

Archetype:
The Elegant Bohemian.

Celebrity:
Julia Louis-Dreyfus, Julianna Margulies.

Motto:
"One step at a time."

Secret Superpower:
When these elegant bohemians offer an invitation, it's hard to resist, whether they're inviting you to lunch, an unexpected weekend in Italy, or a whirlwind romance.

Kryptonite:

This type's kryptonite is stress overload: She's her own worst enemy. She looks elegant as she saunters from home to work to the gym to a night on the town, but she can trip herself in her own velvet cloak.

Nature Image:

Queen Anne's lace, liatris, leptospermum, ombré roses.

Artist:

Jean-Baptiste-Camille Corot.

Charming Contrasts:

Sticking to medium-contrast looks is best for the Elegant Bohemian. A blouse in her version of white with a corset-style vest in the darkest shade of her *energy* color worn with a subtle print skirt in her *energy* color and *First Base* is lovely when paired with *First Base* boots.

Fabulous Fabrics:

Painted velvet, washed silk crepe, brushed moleskin, washed suede.

Signature Scents:

Patchouli, earthy but powdery.

Must-Haves:

The Sunset Summer is an Elegant Bohemian, so she looks terrific in a long cape-style cloak, gaucho pants, a full-sleeved embroidered blouse, a long ribbed-knit skirt, and an off-the-shoulder dress with a drawstring detail at the neckline. These clothes suit both the "elegant" and the "bohemian" sides of her Archetype. She is best in low-key yet lush frills, featuring such old-fashioned details as lace-up plackets, ruffles, and hand embroidery. This Elegant Bohemian looks great in clothes that

have the air of costumes, as long as they're not too flamboyant:
a corset and a long skirt, perhaps, or a poet blouse and a
vestlet.

Must-Avoids:

Clothing that weighs her down or undermines her free-spirited
nature. She should also pass on tailored suits and Hawaiian-
print beachwear, which are neither elegant nor bohemian. A
sharply tailored suit looks oppressive and forced on her, so if she
must wear one to work, let her resist the stiff look with a loose,
carefree hairstyle. On the other hand, Hawaiian-print beachwear
is too high-energy and sporty to suit this smoldering beauty
with a wanderer's heart. Clothing that is not lush and romantic
does not capture her Old World spirit.

Personality and Spirit:

The Sunset Summer is generous, sensitive, and sympathetic.
She's also a very tactile person. She learns a lot from touching
and she communicates with her touch as well. Possessed of
a deep inner serenity and a strong spiritual nature, she often
inspires a profound trust. This trust is absolutely warranted,
for the Sunset Summer can offer you total discretion and will
always keep her word. She's a kind of gardener who tends to
people, ideas, and relationships alike. She throws a terrific party
because she's so sensitive to everyone's needs, which makes her
one of the most hospitable hostesses you're ever likely to meet.
Because the event is so personalized and from her heart, this
may be the most enjoyable party that you have attended in a
very long time. In some lights, the Elegant Bohemian appears
almost mystical, attuned to forces that the rest of us can only
dimly sense. She never tries to be the center of attention but
somehow she's always noticed. She is not lazy in the least,
but neither is she at all competitive; in fact, she'll probably

withdraw from any contest that becomes too drawn out if she senses ugliness brewing. In her book, withdrawing means she has won. She'll go on to find another reward for which she doesn't have to compete.

4. Dusky Summer

Archetype:
The Earth Mother.

Celebrities:
Maggie Gyllenhaal, Meredith Vieira.

Motto:
"I can help you make that better."

Superpower:
This is the woman who brings out the best in everyone. What else are Earth Mothers for?

Kryptonite:
People who don't want help, don't realize they need help, or just don't want to change their situation can drive the Dusky Summer wild with frustration. She just doesn't get it—how can anyone not want to improve?

Nature Image:
Hydrangea, viburnum, ranunculus.

Artist:
Maxfield Parrish.

Charming Contrasts:
The Earth Mother's textures should already absorb and reflect light, so they need a very low contrast. A pastel

romantic-colored dress under a *romantic*-colored coat is simply gorgeous on the Dusky Summer, with a "wow factor" in the gentle beauty of gentle contrasts. Think of her head to toe as the shading of a petal, with each color softly fading into the next.

Fabulous Fabrics:
Anything that's soft and fleecy or simply soft—think cashmere, angora, cotton cashmere, cotton knit.

Signature Scents:
Sandalwood, rose.

Must-Haves:
The Earth Mother looks wonderful in a hooded cashmere wrap jacket, slim knit trousers, a casual gym-inspired drawstring skirt, a tunic-length sweater with a matching tank, and a portrait-collar dress in wool jersey. These clothes seem warm, welcoming, and profoundly at ease.

Must-Avoids:
Harsh, "masculine" styles such as olive-khaki combat-style pants or stiff wool double-breasted suit jackets, as well as any garment made of satin. No matter how in style a double-breasted jacket might be, no matter how perfect the fabric and color, this type of garment on this woman will feel like a straitjacket, masculine and restrictive, and it's likely to grab and ride up when she takes the chair for that important freelance job interview. She is best in clothes that move with her; in fact, clothing that doesn't move actually creates a distraction for her. As for the satin, Dusky Summer's luster is gentle, whereas the luster of satin is not. Dusky Summers also need caressable fabrics. Clothing made of highly reflective materials such as

satin convey a feeling of abrasion and unrest for the Earth
Mother, who has probably spent years buying clothes based on
their tactile quality.

Personality and Spirit:
This mellow Earth Mother likes nothing better than to see
people grow, flourish, and come into their own. She won't do
your work for you, but she'll nurture you to the nth degree
as long as you do your share. The Dusky Summer depends on
having balance in her life, especially between work and time
to de-stress. For this woman, "I go to work and then relax at
home" will never offer enough room to decompress—she
needs a career that has some built-in downtime or better
yet, one that allows her to work at home, where she can
incorporate the ebb and flow of daily life into her work
process. The Earth Mother impulses of the Dusky Summer
reach beyond her immediate circle to anyone she imagines is
in need of a helping hand. No one is more supportive of her
community than she is, whether that support takes the form
of participating in a neighborhood cleanup, volunteering
at a local soup kitchen, or something as simple as making
a donation to charity. One of the ways the Dusky Summer
nourishes herself is by finding beauty in what others often
find ordinary. She will be transported by the simple elegance
of a wood grain or the warm mix of coloring on the front
paw of a shelter dog. Unlike some of her Summer sisters, the
Dusky Summer won't necessarily share these perceptions with
you. Although she is always ready to give and give and give
some more, her unique vision may be the one gift she keeps
for herself.

5 · Renaissance Summer

Archetype:
The Drama Queen.

Celebrities:
Cate Blanchett, Greta Garbo.

Motto:
"I go after what I want—and look fabulous doing it."

Secret Superpower:
She's fearless. Let other people hang back and worry about
how they look, what other people think, what might not turn
out well. The Renaissance Summer rushes in where others
fear to tread—and somehow she makes it work.

Kryptonite:
When this Drama Queen is riding high, she's full of energy,
enthusiasm, and brio—but when she's low, she's *very* low.

Nature Image:
Ranunculus, scabiosa.

Artist:
Peter Paul Rubens.

Charming Contrasts:
The Drama Queen needs to incorporate contrast gently into
her outfit. For example, a tapestry-like pattern offers the
punctuation of contrast and allows her to pull all the different
elements of her outfit together, such as a coat embroidered
in the colors of the blouse and skirt worn underneath. She
should therefore avoid any pattern that is *not* woven into
the fabric. The contrasted vibrancy of printed pattern is

in opposition to the Renaissance Summer's rich oil-paint palette, which is based upon subtlety and gentle color nuances comprised of shades, shadows, and textures.

Fabulous Fabrics:
Suede, burn-out velvet, brocade, corduroy, lawn. The Renaissance Summer is at her best when swathed in texture. Think Renaissance tapestry. The richer the fabric, the more beautiful she looks. These rich fabrics and their subtle light play will flatter and accentuate the textures of her skin and hair.

Signature Scents:
Black currant, pine.

Must-Haves:
The Drama Queen favors period clothing with a dramatic flair: a long, fitted single-breasted velvet coat, a peasant blouse with a wide belt, slim legging-type trousers tucked into tall boots, a long suede skirt, a poet-inspired blouse with lace cuffs, and a dress featuring corset detailing. Her wardrobe relies on patterns, textures, and lightly woven fabrics, set off by the rich blended palette of deep browns, burgundies, and teals that bring her Renaissance looks to life. Clothes that have gentle movement, such as an ankle-length sweater coat worn with tall suede boots or an extra-long skinny scarf cowled around her neck, set her off to perfection. Her wedding gown should be corset-style, evoking the grandeur of an Elizabethan monarch. Think of a corset worn with a layered chiffon skirt. The corset braces the silhouette and emphasizes her strong femininity, and the flowing chiffon reveals her soft damsel-in-distress side, evoking the image of a princess in a tower, longing for a chivalrous suitor.

Must-Avoids:

Pedestrian or "basic" clothing. No one looks worse in jeans
and a plain T-shirt than the Renaissance Summer. The plainer
the clothing, the harsher she looks. And this is a shame,
because our Drama Queen is not in the least harsh-looking.
She just does not look contemporary but rather has the look
of another time. Consequently the Renaissance Summer
should pass on overalls—too many hard edges and seams, and
because they are based upon men's work wear, they're too
pedestrian and mundane.

Personality and Spirit:

No doubt about it, the Renaissance Summer is a force to
be reckoned with. This Drama Queen has her diva side,
using her feminine wiles to get what she wants, but her sexy,
sensual persona ensures that she usually achieves any goal
she sets. She's fiercely loyal and she'll maintain an alliance
longer than any of the other *Archetypes.* No one thinks
more quickly on her feet than she does, and no one keeps
her balance better, either. If the other Summer types are
in the context of the elements, the Renaissance Summer
is earth: She operates close to the ground, giving a whole
new meaning to the phrase "down to earth." Whereas most
Summers resemble watercolors, the Renaissance Summer is
painted in rich, sensuous oils that resemble a gentler version
of Autumn.

6. Iridescent Summer

Archetype:

The Mysterious Mermaid.

Celebrities:
Leelee Sobieski, Meryl Streep, Uma Thurman.

Motto:
"I can help you make your dreams come true."

Secret Superpower:
From throwing an elaborate surprise party to creating a gift
basket for a neighbor in the hospital, the Mysterious Mermaid
makes lovely things happen in an effortless, almost magical
way. You might almost suspect her of getting up early in the
morning or slipping away after bedtime to accomplish all her
extra tasks, as though she has a whole other life that no one
else is privy to. . . .

Kryptonite:
People who don't believe in possibility and dreams. The
Mysterious Mermaid will stop at nothing to help a friend
fulfill her heart's desire, but she can't bear to be around people
who have given up on all of life's wonderful possibilities.

Nature Image:
Bluebells or lily of the valley—anything small, delicate, elfin.

Artists:
Rosalba Carriera and some of the brighter works of Georges
Seurat.

Charming Contrasts:
Dress the Mysterious Mermaid in low-contrast shades that
blend together from head to toe. Think water-colored ombré
effects or a top and bottom in contrasting tones of the same
color, with a long scarf that has both colors in it, set off by
some iridescent silver, of course!

Fabulous Fabrics:
Iridescent chiffon, pearlized leather, crewel knit, delicately embroidered calf—again, this mysterious creature does best in translucent, shimmery fabrics.

Signature Scents:
White narcissus, or anything crisp and delicate. Careful, though—white linen is *too* crisp.

Must-Haves:
This Mysterious Mermaid needs clothes as mysterious and shimmery as her signature coloring. She favors a leather asymmetrical jacket with an iridescent luster, slim stretch jeans, a beaded tunic-style blouse, a seamed chiffon corkscrew-style skirt, and a sari-inspired gown: delicate, lustrous, dreamy, and magical. The Iridescent Summer is almost fairylike, and her colors should always be light, dusky, and translucent, like gossamer wings. Just think of the way flowers, leaves, and branches look on a dewy summer morning. Her clothes need to be flowy and uninterrupted. She looks terrific in a long scarf, which lengthens her silhouette and maintains her magical flow. The Mysterious Mermaid would look terrific in jewelry or accessories made of art glass. A raincoat made of pearlized canvas is fantastic for her as well. The Mysterious Mermaid looks fabulous in ballet flats, but she should never wear heavy-soled boots, which weigh down this light and airy creature.

Must-Avoids:
Any outfit comprised of too many lines, such as a short jacket with a blouse peeking out or trousers tucked into tall boots. Such a silhouette is too jagged and severe for our Mysterious Mermaid, who needs to be swathed in gently flowing garments. The Iridescent Summer should make sure

to pass on taffeta ball gowns and patch pockets. Though taffeta has a luster that suits this type, the stiff noisy effect contrasts unpleasantly with her role as a herder or shepherdess to those around her. The swish of taffeta seems harsh and abrasive on her . . . and the sheep would be easily frightened by it! Patch pockets, meanwhile, not only interrupt the Iridescent Summer's fluid head-to-toe silhouette but somehow suggest that she has hidden secrets. Nothing could be more incorrect for this type. She is straightforward, light-handed, and what you see is exactly what you get: She may not reveal everything about herself on a first date, but I guarantee that on Date Five you will still find her as captivating as on Date One and have found that your first impression was entirely accurate!

Personality and Spirit:

The Iridescent Summer has a magical eldritch quality—her *Archetype* might be equally the Mermaid, the Fairy, or the Sprite. You'll know her by her marvelous light laugh, which never fails to inspire laughter among everyone within earshot. She has the rare ability to listen to a loved one's problems, understand fully and deeply, and then do everything in her power to put the other person in the line of possibility. She never directly scolds or even instructs, but only inspires and supports in her nonjudgmental way. She never offers help for her own satisfaction but only in a truly selfless way. Despite her willingness to inspire, though, she feels awkward being asked a direct question; the Mysterious Mermaid always prefers the oblique route. Though the Iridescent Summer definitely adores her downtime, she's willing to put quite a few hours in to helping her friends, neighbors, and colleagues. She has the gift of being able to corral a group together, but gently, never in a forceful way.

Autumn

1. Spicy Autumn

Archetype:
The Sensuous Backpacker.

Celebrities:
Joy Behar, Sandra Bullock, Hilary Swank, Nia Vardalos.

Motto:
"Have an adventure every day!"

Secret Superpower:
Bringing many diverse ingredients into a harmonious whole.
If you need someone to coordinate a team at work, to pull
together the elements of an outfit, or to figure out how to
select food, dishes, centerpieces, and background music to
create the perfect dinner party, just ask the Spicy Autumn.

Kryptonite:
Injustice. The Spicy Autumn likes to work hard and play hard,
but nothing saps her energy like an encounter with a situation
or person that she deems unfair. Injustice simply rattles her.

Nature Image:
Hypericum, sunflower, red ginger.

Artist:
Paul Gauguin.

Charming Contrasts:
This Sensuous Backpacker has the most blended overall look
of all the types. Think of a bowl on your kitchen counter into

which you have poured several herbs and spices. A simple *energy*-colored sweater and ***Third Base*** trousers will be blah and boring on the Spicy Autumn unless she adds an exotic hand-forged necklace to bring the pants' color up into her whole head-to-toe look.

Fabulous Fabrics:
Patterned velvet, leather, brushed denim, crêpe.

Signature Scents:
Clove, cumin.

Must-Haves:
This type favors an embroidered three-quarter-length coat, boot-cut corduroy trousers, a batik-printed camisole, a sari-style wrap skirt, and a mandarin-style dress. Think of her outfits as a delicious casserole or stew, incorporating a palette of spicy hues and a multitude of exotic flavors into a satisfying blend. As you observe the rich colors hanging in her closet, you can almost smell the saffron, ginger, and cayenne. On any other type, the muddy browns and grayish greens that she favors would look dull as dishwater, but on our Sensuous Backpacker, they evoke olive groves and steamy jungles. She gets the most bang for her buck out of muted colors made mysterious and dramatic through the mix of patterns and textures, which create a brooding, sultry quality that can be quite enticing. No other type has her flair for ethnic styles and unusual accessories. She's the perfect type to mix a batik print with an angora sweater and a piece of wooden jewelry, and somehow, she makes those contrasts work. The Spicy Autumn adds dimension to her palette through the play of textures and colors. Her clothing silhouettes should all be based on swift practical lines and her

ideal style incorporates global influences from many different cultures.

Must-Avoids:

The Sensuous Backpacker should pass on perky full-skirted dresses and all ruffles not cut with pinking shears and shredded. If you were to observe the Spicy Autumn in a full-skirted dress from a second-floor window, you would see an angular woman surrounded by a circle whose body yearns to be draped in fabric that stretches across her hips and thighs in a more rugged, sensual, nonsymmetrical manner. The perkiness of the full-circle skirt does not mesh with the woman who is a fighter for justice. Similarly, ruffles seem silly and little-girlish. Details such as large ruffled sleeves or oversized buttons down the front of a jacket are not organic enough for this type, who finds these elements "tacked on" and cartoonish, rather than stemming from a practical purpose.

Personality and Spirit:

The Sensuous Backpacker has an eclectic life full of glorious, unexpected adventure—and a wardrobe made up of things she collects along the way. Yet although she makes herself at home wherever she goes, her real home and hearth are very important to the Spicy Autumn. If the Spicy Autumn's surroundings are in order, she feels in order; otherwise, she's often uneasy without knowing why. The Spicy Autumn is warm and nurturing, but her emotions are surprisingly close to the surface, and if something is on her mind, she can't not say it. Always, however, this type is very kind, with a generosity that can surprise you.

2. Mellow Autumn

Archetype:
The Sexy Librarian.

Celebrities:
Diane Lane, Emma Thompson, Kate Winslet.

Motto:
"I do the right thing for its own sake."

Secret Superpower:
Despite her mellow exterior, the Mellow Autumn slices through a problem with a surgeon's scalpel. She sees straight to the heart of any issue, almost at a glance. You almost feel that you could show her a Rubik's cube and she could figure out the solution without even touching it.

Kryptonite:
Being thrust into the spotlight. The Mellow Autumn works best behind the scenes.

Nature Image:
Freesia, Fuji mum, Ixia.

Artist:
Jan Vermeer.

Charming Contrasts:
The Sexy Librarian's look requires relatively low contrast but with some drama in her shape and composition. The best use of contrast is a very artistic **Third Base** dress worn with **First Base** shoes and tights, one focal piece of jewelry that makes a statement, and a bag in either her **First Base** or **Third Base,** so the piece of jewelry—and its wearer—are the focal point. The

Mellow Autumn needs to make sure she doesn't clutter her landscape.

Fabulous Fabrics:
Harris tweed, China silk, handkerchief linen, bouclé.

Signature Scents:
Musk, eucalyptus.

Must-Haves:
What else would you expect the Sexy Librarian to wear but a suede trench coat, 1940s-style tweed trousers, a pleated twill blouse with three-quarter sleeves and shoulder placket, a topstitched A-line paneled skirt, and a metallic knit shift dress with twisted straps—all clothes with an image of propriety and a sexy flair. You may often see the Sexy Librarian in a hipped-up "bookish" outfit. But don't underestimate her fashion smarts: She might also surprise you by attending, say, a wedding in an extremely modern dress, something that on a hanger in the store most people would not have the capacity to understand, let alone to try it on and purchase it. She will wear this cutting-edge garment with full confidence—and because she understands what the dress is all about, she'll be able to pull off a daring new look that some of her seemingly more stylish sisters would never even attempt.

Must-Avoids:
The Mellow Autumn looks terrific in clothes that *seem* severe, but she should pass on high-contrast prints that *are* severe. Her time of day is twilight, when the setting of the sun creates a soft merging of the colors found in a country garden—no harsh sunlight or cool moonlight, so only gentle contrasts, please. And on her, the chiffon bow blouse will seem relentlessly asexual, so she should pass on that, too. That large

bow limply hanging down the front of a blouse or dress feels ridiculous and childlike for this type: She's instantly annoyed by its lack of purpose. Instead, she's excited by purposeful design, holding in great regard for those who figure out a way to make the mundane artistically pleasing.

Personality and Spirit:

The Sexy Librarian may look terrific in her clingy suede skirt and trim blazer, but she'd be the last one to notice how good she looks: She's the least vain of all the *Archetypes*— and, perhaps, the hardest worker to boot. If she weren't so irreverent and fun, her *Archetype* would be the Girl Scout, because she's *such* a good scout: loyal, devoted, industrious, and always ready to put work before play. She's not just smart, she's an intellectual—analytical, incisive—but don't underestimate her razor-sharp wit and wicked sense of humor. This soulful woman is a solid citizen but she's also got a great streak of irony that can surprise even the people who know her best.

3. Gamine Autumn

Archetype:

The Stylish Beatnik.

Celebrities:

Jessica Biel, Tovah Feldshuh, Sarah Jessica Parker, Jada Pinkett Smith.

Motto:

"I do it my way."

Secret Superpower:

Her unique and intensely personal process. If you want

someone who does things like no one else, go to the Gamine Autumn—you'll never confuse her with anybody else.

Kryptonite:
Trying to blend in. She can't do it. She shouldn't try. This type's forte is doing her own thing, and as long as she's allowed to be her own unique self, she'll shine as brightly as she deserves to. But when she's asked to blend in, she becomes fierce, fiery, and bad-tempered.

Nature Image:
Seeded eucalyptus, Lenten rose.

Artists:
Frans Hals, Albrecht Dürer.

Charming Contrasts:
This atypical Stylish Beatnik looks best in medium contrast, so if she's going to wear more than one color at a time, she should turn to prints. A medium-contrast paisley print summer dress comprised of her *essence, romantic,* and *Second Base* colors is best offset by sandals, a shoulder bag, and jewelry in her *Second Base.*

Fabulous Fabrics:
Silk dupioni, muslin, basket cloth, raw silk.

Signature Scents:
Rose oil, cedar.

Must-Haves:
This Stylish Beatnik looks terrific in a hooded overcoat with toggles, stirrup leggings, a tie-front blouse worn under a jumper, a pencil skirt with buttons up the side, and a fine-wale corduroy shirtdress. This lady is quixotic, and the unusual

delights her beyond belief. Her wedding gown will not be a wedding gown at all, but a short stylish dress most certainly in a color other than white . . . possibly worn with a smart little chapeau that she has custom-designed herself. And she would look terrific in a dress made of light-handed tweed and accessorized with items such as a bouclé cloche hat or a pair of whip-stitched gloves—playful styles and accessories that express her singular, youthful personality. Or you might see her in a cute little sixties shift dress with a beret, maybe with a unique, handmade necklace and a one-of-a-kind set of earrings. She almost can't help developing a signature style, perhaps built around a unique conversation piece such as a vintage handbag or a special pin that she wears on her favorite coat.

Must-Avoids:
Anything ordinary or, heaven forbid, classic. The simple little black dress does nothing for this unconventional type and she should avoid it like the plague. This Gamine Autumn should make sure to pass on solid color sheath dresses and floor-length anything. A solid gabardine sheath dress looks sexy on some women but staid on this one, as it constricts her quirkiness. And no chiffon, please, because that fabric, while soft and sexy, has no "pluck," a signature quality of the Gamine Autumn. She needs clothing that illustrates her marvelous humor and her eclectic interests. Her plucky quick-witted energy is contrasted with anything that drags on the floor or trails.

Personality and Spirit:
If you're looking for a stellar team player—someone who's loyal, hardworking, and absolutely dedicated—the Gamine Autumn is your woman. She has an extraordinary ability to balance her unconventional style with a disciplined commitment to the group's larger goals. Although she needs to

be given the freedom to do things in her own way, she never seeks the limelight. She wants attention—but only as part of the team. The Stylish Beatnik has a certain amount of visibility in her social circle—people definitely remember having met her. But she also tends to be a highly private person. With those few intimates she really trusts, she'll share her heart's secrets, but many people who consider themselves among her closest friends would be surprised to find how little they really know her. The Gamine Autumn brings her off-beat sense of style to her daily life, where she lives in her own special, theatrical way. Whether she's telling you about the hot new band she heard last night or creating her own quirky set of fashion trends, she maintains her originality.

4. Copper Autumn

Archetype:
The High Stakes Gambler.

Celebrities:
Rita Hayworth, Katharine Hepburn, Julianne Moore, Jessica Rabbit.

Motto:
"I make my own luck!"

Secret Superpower:
She's totally up-front about what she wants—and she often gets it.

Kryptonite:
Not getting her own way. Of course, no one likes not getting her own way. But for the Copper Autumn, being crossed,

frustrated, or even unreasonably delayed just pushes her buttons. That's when you see her vulnerability—her coppery flame goes out and until she finds a way to refuel, she's just not open for business.

Nature Image:
Pincushion protea, parakeet heliconia.

Artist:
Paul Cezanne.

Charming Contrasts:
The High Stakes Gambler has a natural sense of drama, but that doesn't mean she's looking for a high-contrast ensemble. In fact, low contrasts work better for her coloring, and she should look to her metals as a way of pulling together the different shades in her outfits. She's lucky in that metallic clothing works for day as well as evening wear, so that a copper knit sweater is a perfect casual accessory worn with *Second Base* fine-wale corduroy slacks.

Fabulous Fabrics:
Taffeta, shantung, sari, challis.

Signature Scents:
Marigold, grapefruit.

Must-Haves:
What's the ideal wardrobe for a High Stakes Gambler? A mandarin-style brocade coat, slim velvet stretch pants, a ribbed turtleneck, a high-waisted pencil skirt, and a taffeta fit-and-flare party dress. Feisty, passionate, and daring, she needs clothes that allow her to stride through life while looking as though she can well afford to be at the high stakes table.

Must-Avoids:

Royal blue and red orange—even though she may love those colors. But the coolness of royal blue washes her out and the orange is too heavy and hard for her, especially since it clashes with the reds in her hair. And our Copper Autumn should pass on drop-waist dresses and polo shirts. This feisty type needs to have a tight-fitted waist in all her clothing, as if to remind her of her strong, rooted base. On her, a dropped waist looks careless, and you might even see her posture droop to match the character of the dress. Polo shirts on this lady look like a uniform, and a logo makes the effect for her even worse. Why, she might want to know, should she be advertising someone *else's* brand, when her own is so fascinating?

Personality and Spirit:

By some accounts, this High Stakes Gambler is what you might call a hothead—in a totally sultry, glamorous way, of course. As befits a High Stakes Gambler, the Copper Autumn is adventurous, tenacious, and forthright. Usually, the Copper Autumn is good at asking for exactly what she wants in both love and work. "I would really appreciate a conversation with you about my future at the company and a possible promotion," she might say. Or perhaps, "I've loved these last few months, but now we need to talk about where this relationship is going." Nothing in her life happens by chance or coincidence: She makes it happen. She's strong, sure of herself, willing to take risks—and she won't take no for an answer.

5. Bronze Autumn

Archetype:
The Divine Diva.

Celebrities:
Cindy Crawford, Angelina Jolie, Sophia Loren, Oprah
Winfrey.

Motto:
"I'm fabulous—and so are you!"

Secret Superpower:
Making the mundane seem fabulous. Follow this Divine Diva
to a staff meeting, and you'll think it's a party. Join her at the
gym, and you'll thrill to the joy of movement. The Bronze
Autumn makes even a trip to the grocery store come alive
with unexpected possibilities.

Kryptonite:
Not being noticed. The Divine Diva thrives when all eyes are
upon her—but when threatened with obscurity, she wilts and
will probably excuse herself.

Nature Image:
Gloriosa lily, anthurium.

Artist:
Gustav Klimt.

Charming Contrasts:
The dramatic coloring of the Divine Diva calls for high
contrast, so if she *does* want to wear a monochromatic outfit,
she must employ a lot of texture. An ensemble in her ***First
Base*** can work—but only if she adds exotic earrings, a fur

collar, or a suede belt; otherwise her outfit is too harsh, cold, and uniform-like.

Fabulous Fabrics:
Charmeuse, Persian lamb, Chinese brocade, linen.

Signature Scents:
Mandarin orange, fig.

Must-Haves:
Oh, how divine is this Divine Diva, in her long wool coat with an oversized faux-fur collar, mandarin-style trousers, burnout velvet fitted blouse with slit sleeves, skirt with an asymmetrical hem, and long-sleeved plunging-neckline jersey dress reminiscent of a Martha Graham dance costume. These long-line, asymmetrical, dashing clothes suit her flamboyant, dramatic nature, telling the world at a glance that here is a woman who knows how to make *everyone* feel fabulous. The drama in her nature is reflected in her clothing, but it's a luxe drama that does not seem to try hard to grab attention. When she shops, she might think, "This look is perfectly me, and I can't imagine another person being able to carry this off!" With her natural presence and expressive personality, her clothing should flatter her like a sumptuous backdrop in a Verdi opera flatters and supports the singer in front of it. Her clothing is grand and well chosen but never upstages her.

Must-Avoids:
The Bronze Autumn should be sure to pass on cap sleeves and anything made of denim. Cap sleeves come off as cutesy, acting as a punctuation pop on the shoulder line. This Divine Diva doesn't need her clothing to provide popping punctuation, though, and cap sleeves only compete with her

marvelous presence. Denim and similar cottons don't work on her, either: They just don't have the right texture to suit the richness of her palette.

Personality and Spirit:

Exotic is the word that comes to mind when you see a Bronze Autumn, though *flamboyant* probably runs a close second. When this Divine Diva strides into the room, a loud gong strikes as if to say, "She has arrived!" At least, that's what the Divine Diva tends to hear, and she's got the charisma, flair, and panache to make everybody else hear it, too. For the Bronze Autumn, life is always full of drama and always marvelous. She can make even the most mundane event seem special. "Oh, darling," she might enthuse, "I saw the most *wonderful* orange at the greengrocer and brought it here—just for you!" And somehow, in her hands, that ordinary little orange turns into an exotic delicacy. The Divine Diva is the type of woman who can make you believe that she deserves the word *Countess* before her first name. Dress her in the sexy, brilliant clothes that are her due, and watch her light up the stage. You'll never have a better time at any show.

6. High Autumn

Archetype:

The Passionate Impresario.

Celebrity:

Jodie Foster, Felicity Huffman.

Motto:

"Life is a banquet!"

Secret Superpower:

Extra-high energy. If you're looking for someone who approaches life with boundless enthusiasm and an unlimited supply of vitality, get the High Autumn on your team.

Kryptonite:

Committing to a project out of a sense of obligation rather than interest. Because the High Autumn is so high-energy when she's excited about a project, her friends and colleagues—and even she herself—can lose sight of what happens when she's not genuinely moved to act. This type has limitless energy—until she loses interest.

Nature Image:

Bird of paradise, tiger lily.

Artist:

Henri de Toulouse-Lautrec.

Charming Contrasts:

The high-energy Passionate Impresario needs a vivid high-contrast look—as long as the contrast is rooted in her outfit. For example, a *romantic*-colored V-neck sweater against a *Second Base* tweed skirt works best if the tweed is shot with slubs of the *romantic* color. Otherwise, the outfit won't be theatrical enough and on her will look too much like catering staff attire.

Fabulous Fabrics:

Irish tweed, quilted silk satin, damask, embroidered linen.

Signature Scent:

Amber.

Must-Haves:

The Passionate Impresario's style is asymmetrical and apparently disharmonious, with colors that nobody else would dream of putting together. She favors a blazer in the style of a smoking jacket, mandarin-style trousers, a high-necked blouse with a dramatic collar, a skirt with an asymmetrical hem, and a one-shoulder cashmere knit sweater gown. Her quiet dignity and authority are set off by clothes like these, which also give the nod to her theatrical nature and dramatic flair. This type lives life on her terms and should dress accordingly. She is all about a play of textures or gentle patterns which somehow rise to the level of flamboyance. If she feels protected and armored by an absolutely fantastic outfit, she will make her entrance into any party fully confident and will then have a marvelous time.

Must-Avoids:

The High Autumn needs to pass on basic suits and anything that seems too conventional. True, she can flourish in a corporate environment as long as there are constant challenges, but she should never think of her clothing as a uniform. She should wear only suits she feels look great on her, and they'll probably be unusual in some detail of style or cut. Consequently, if the High Autumn wears clothing that is simple and nontheatrical, it won't seem like "enough" on her.

Personality and Spirit:

No one loves a new beginning like a High Autumn. To this feisty lady, the first step of any new project, relationship, or adventure is always a thrill. If she's allowed to race through the experience, she'll do just fine; her frustration comes when she's required to go back and fill in the details. She needs new, exciting, and demanding challenges to hold her attention, though fortunately, she excels at creating such new experiences for herself. There is no *no* for the High Autumn— what she goes after, she gets. The High Autumn's passion might lead some to think she's unfocused, but nothing could be further from the truth. She's supercommitted to anything she takes on. She just needs to make sure that she's committing out of interest, not out of obligation.

Winter

1. Classic Winter

Archetype:
The Queen.

Celebrities:
Zooey Deschanel, Penélope Cruz, Anne Hathaway, Sandra Oh.

Motto:
"There's a natural order to everything."

Secret Superpower:
Her grace can be inspirational to others.

Kryptonite:
Vulgarity makes her skin crawl.

Nature Image:
Red roses.

Artist:
Diego Velázquez.

Charming Contrasts:
No one wears simple high contrast better than the Queen.
A gown that features her version of white in the bodice, her
version of black in the skirt, and a sash in her *romantic* color is
breathtaking. Only a pair of earrings in a clear stone should be
worn with this look or it might become heavy.

Fabulous Fabrics:
Lace, gabardine, matte satin, mohair, georgette.

Signature Scents:
Wintergreen, carnation.

Must-Haves:
All hail the Queen, in her dolman-sleeve single-breasted
jacket, unpleated moderate-leg trousers, bateau-neck knit
sweater, suede pencil skirt, and 1960s-style shift dress. She can
look majestic when she dresses up and quietly regal in her
lovely, casual garments. Her lines need to be simple but never
harsh.

Must-Avoids:
This lovely lady should pass on anything that says "I am
a silly gal" or "I am unapproachable." Unless worn with a
tremendous amount of irony for a costume party, a printed
T-shirt of cartoon characters looks completely out of place on
the Queen, as though she were wearing an evening gown to
a fast-food restaurant. While irony is definitely an important
part of her personality, she should never access it through her
clothing, but rather through her words and laughter. She must

take extra care when shopping because many of the items that she will be drawn to in a store may teeter on the edge of being just a bit too harsh for her. She should think of her wardrobe as "classic and elegant" and not as "body armor." Also, she should take care never to look fussy—or as though she's been dressed by a single designer. Finally, although no one looks better in the little black dress, she should make sure to experience the other colors on her palette, too, so that she can express her inner nature and open herself up to different facets of her personality.

Personality and Spirit:

The Classic Winter gives new meaning to the word *regal*. Even when she's wearing jeans and a sweatshirt, she makes you feel as though you're hanging out with a member of the royal family. She's never pretentious and this lady can crack a joke, but no matter how relaxed she seems, she still exudes a natural poise that somehow connotes royalty. The Classic Winter's Queen-like nature makes her strong, competent, and regal. She has a deep, soulful quality on which she draws, enabling her to disregard the petty and the trivial to focus on the issues, tasks, and people that really matter. The Classic Winter is also quite logical and supplements her sense of tradition with the keen insights of a rational, incisive mind. But let's not ignore the Queen's often wicked sense of humor and her pleasure in physical activities. Her sexy, sensuous side comes out in any situation where manners, elegance, and grace can provide the boundaries and the form she needs.

2. Soft Winter

Archetype:
The Romantic Poetess.

Celebrities:
Joan Collins, Jennifer Connelly, Christina Ricci, Elizabeth Taylor.

Motto:
"When I want to know the truth, I look within."

Secret Superpower:
The soft-spoken Soft Winter commands a subtle but unmistakable respect from her friends, loved ones, and colleagues. When she gives her blessing to something, everyone breathes a sigh of relief and goes ahead.

Kryptonite:
Anything harsh, jarring, or out of tune: The wrong note on a piano could ruin her day. She's almost hypersensitive to any type of deception in a situation, a person, or a relationship—and she finds deception extremely demoralizing.

Nature Image:
White camellia.

Artists:
William Merritt Chase, Sir Thomas Lawrence, Thomas Sully.

Charming Contrasts:
The Romantic Poetess needs to wear shades of the same color in different textures, and using different costume-y silhouettes is stunning for this type. Pairing several shades of her ***Third Base,*** such as a cashmere turtleneck, suede belt, skirt, and

boots with a long Nehru-collared coat, creates a dramatic yet soft effect.

Fabulous Fabrics:
Velvet, satin-faced wool, French lace, cotton batiste.

Signature Scent:
Vanilla.

Must-Haves:
The Romantic Poetess looks lovely in a long suede duster, washed silk poet blouse, long ribbed-knit skirt, fluid crepe trousers without pockets or waistband, and a velvet plunge dress. These romantic garments suit the soft-spoken Soft Winter, who needs a gentler line than her Winter sisters. As the most romantic of all the Winters, this woman's lush spirit is set off by a simple cream-colored Empire gown, and she wears a cameo like no one else. Nothing suits her more than the look of an old-fashioned painting.

Must-Avoids:
The color yellow. Also anything jagged, such as an asymmetrical skirt or a peaked lapel jacket. Forget about anything rustic—she's too sophisticated. And the Soft Winter should definitely stay away from any hard line—the oval is her shape. Our Soft Winter should also pass on the leather pants and the hippie chic, for sure. Leather jeans are too abrasive for her gentle nature, and the almost strident luster of the fabric coupled with a jean cut in will make her appear to stomp instead of glide. The Soft Winter's trousers need to flow with the natural curves of her legs—a look she'll never get with leather. Finally, while there is a mellow, soulful quality to this type, the hippie chic look is too cluttered and not refined enough for her, as she is quite precise in her choices.

This sense of order must translate into her clothing and her surroundings.

Personality and Spirit:
The Soft Winter has a quiet power that everyone around her feels even if few understand it. Her approval almost feels like a priestess's blessing, because the soft radiance of her deeply spiritual nature extends to everyone in her presence. The Romantic Poetess is so in tune with her own feelings and with the feelings of others that at times it almost seems as though she's psychic. Perhaps her greatest gift is self-knowledge, a gift she's earned through a slow, steady tending of her spiritual gifts. Her whole life is about growing and learning, especially about herself. The Soft Winter is found attractive by everyone she comes in contact with. She's romantic, rather than sexually overt, and relationships with her need time to build. Because she's highly sensitive, her feelings can be hurt very easily. But she also knows how to use her sensitivity to tune in to the emotional undercurrents that often prevail in personal and professional situations, enhancing her effectiveness in both work and love. Though everything about the Soft Winter seems completely harmonious, she will often have one unexpected quirk, such as a love of heavy-metal music or league bowling. That modern touch combined with her dreamy, romantic nature makes her beguiling in a very special way.

3. Dynamic Winter

Archetype:
The Passionate Leader.

Celebrities:
Linda Dano, Teri Hatcher, Mary Steenburgen, Rachel Weisz.

Motto:
"I know what's needed and I'll make sure it happens."

Secret Superpower:
Natural authority. When she knows what's right, everyone
recognizes the truth that she sees and willingly—even
eagerly—follows her lead.

Kryptonite:
When people doubt her authority, the Dynamic Winter often
starts to question herself.

Nature Image:
White calla lilies.

Artist:
Josiah Copley.

Charming Contrasts:
Our Passionate Leader should wear high-contrast outfits
without cutting up her body head to toe. A dynamic effect can
be created using a color where a neutral is usually used, such
as taking a *dramatic*-colored dress and pairing it with *First
Base* jewelry, purse, shoes, and coat. The lines of her clothing
should always have a theatricality to them, so her basic colors
will be made exciting.

Fabulous Fabrics:
Embossed velvet, pleated chiffon, charmeuse, crisp linen,
cotton poplin.

Signature Scent:
Orchid.

Must-Haves:
Authority plus flair equals the Dynamic Winter in her silver
metallic trench coat, sheer poncho worn over a tank, three-
quarter sari-wrap skirt, fluid, wide-legged three-layer chiffon
trousers, and Chinese satin sheath dress. She needs clothes
that make a strong statement without seeming harsh or
conventional. The Dynamic Winter's colors are clear and sharp,
and her interiors are clean and high contrast. Both her outfits
and her interiors should be vivid, well balanced, and carefully
thought out.

Must-Avoids:
Anything frilly, girly, or insubstantial. The Passionate Leader
should avoid low-contrasted combinations and long hair.
This type needs "pop" and drama in her clothing and her
combinations of colors. Ensembles comprised of several muted
blended colors pull her visual energy down and take away her
power. Contrary to popular belief that long hair is feminine,
long hair in an unlayered cut will actually not feminize the
Dynamic Winter at all. It will simply hang limply in contrast
to her prominent features and actually make her features look
harsher against the soft texture of her hair.

Personality and Spirit:
Cool, calm, and collected, the Dynamic Winter seems all
business when you first meet her, but you'll soon realize that
this Passionate Leader is capable of working magic. Under
her direction, people discover that they're somehow able to
achieve feats far beyond what they ever dreamed of, while
she is working toward a vision that pulls the whole group
together. The Dynamic Winter is somehow able to be both
friendly and authoritative, partly because her natural authority
seems to win her the acknowledgment and confidence usually

accorded to experts. If you walked into a room and saw her in a group of five, you'd immediately assume she was in charge, even if she was the youngest person there. Her poise and perceived intelligence win this Passionate Leader instant respect. She isn't cocky or a show-off; just the kind of person who inspires others to have confidence in themselves— and her. The Dynamic Winter's aura of expertise wins her promotion frequently. She's a quick study and can master just about anything in a surprisingly short amount of time.

4. Vivid Winter

Archetype:
The Earthy Philosopher.

Celebrities:
Keira Knightley, Vanessa Marcil, Catherine Zeta-Jones.

Motto:
"Truth Above All."

Secret Superpower:
When this lady thinks something is her duty, she is unstoppable.

Kryptonite:
Feeling obligated. Although the Vivid Winter will stop at nothing to fulfill obligations she believes she has freely chosen, she is equally determined to avoid any obligations that others try to saddle her with. She'll live up to her own sense of right, but she becomes demoralized if others try to make her feel beholden or—heaven forbid—guilty.

Nature Image:
Poinsettia, white Japanese magnolia.

Artist:
Henri Matisse.

Charming Contrasts:
The Vivid Winter needs a high level of contrast, which means that her total image is more still—and very effective. Her look is best achieved without patterns, and the higher the contrast, the more exciting. Think of a beautiful *tranquil*-colored sweater worn with a *First Base* skirt, coat, purse, and shoes. The *tranquil* color almost serves the role of a pattern to create a "wow" effect.

Fabulous Fabrics:
Cashmere, Persian lamb, satin, Chinese brocade, cotton lawn, silk knit, light cotton knit.

Signature Scents:
Jasmine, licorice.

Must-Haves:
The Earthy Philosopher needs grounded clothes with clear, clean lines. She'll look terrific in a long fit-and-flare alpaca coat, Nehru-collar silk blouse, skirt made of three layers of pleated silk, clean jersey pants, and a matte jersey long-sleeved dress ruched at the bust. As you see, the Vivid Winter has plenty of flair—but she also has a very strong wardrobe. Despite the simplicity of the Vivid Winter's approach, this striking woman can pull off a few costume pieces without looking either eccentric or costume-y. A kimono-style jacket would become her, as would a large, unusual piece of jewelry.

Because of her still, priestesslike quality, she needs a slightly frivolous touch to make her accessible. Left to her own devices, she might end up wearing the same uniform every day—black turtleneck, slacks, a simple pair of earrings—so she's got to make an effort to add some color and flair to bring out her own unique, vivid style. The effort is well worth her while, however, since with just a few small touches, the Vivid Winter can be absolutely stunning.

Must-Avoids:

The Vivid Winter wants to pass on ruffles and sack-style dresses. She is a charming and intellectually stimulating person, and her clothes need to illustrate her spirit. Ruffles are fun and frolicsome and carefree, three words that would never be used for this lovely lady. Sack-style dresses, meanwhile, are shapeless and noncommittal in their form. But the Vivid Winter is never noncommittal in her style or personality, quite the contrary. She's so committed that she finds it perplexing that others need to call to confirm dinner plans the day before.

Personality and Spirit:

The Vivid Winter has an extremely attractive quality, both sexually and as a person who projects a solid, reliable image. One look at this Earthy Philosopher, and you know that you can trust her with your life. She's extremely honest and straightforward, but she's not always easy to read. If you ask her to tell you what she's passionate about, she will, but you might not be able to see it right away. Likewise, if you ask her what she's feeling, she'll be straight with you, but she may tend to conceal her highs and lows behind a cheerful facade. She doesn't intend to deceive you or to hide anything—she just doesn't wear her emotions on the surface. The Earthy Philosopher is not purposely mysterious, but she does believe

in being discreet. She shares information on a strictly need-to-
know basis, and she makes very certain she trusts you before
you're admitted into the inner circle of friends and loved ones
who get to hear how she really feels. Her opinions, on the
other hand, she shares freely and even vehemently, arguing
with a passion that reveals her commitment to the truth.
She doesn't mind admitting she's wrong—though she rarely
believes she is! But finding the truth, rather than being right,
is what matters to this Earthy Philosopher. Her generosity and
loyalty make her popular, even beloved, by both her intimates
and those who have met her only once.

5. Antique Winter

Archetype:
The Keeper of the Hearth.

Celebrity:
Allison Janney. (This type is rarely found front and center in a
national way.)

Motto:
"I'll do the remembering for all of us."

Secret Superpower:
She remembers your most important secret and tells it back to
you just when you need it most.

Kryptonite:
Her gift is remembering the past—but sometimes she has
trouble focusing on the future.

Nature Image:
Seed pod, pieris shrub.

Artist:
James McNeill Whistler.

Charming Contrasts:
Though her contrasts are the gentlest of all of the Winter types, this type wears a bit of print better than any of her Winter sisters—but she needs to use it gently. An embossed fabric in a coat of two shades of the *Third Base* can be a beautiful look over a *Third Base/tranquil* outfit. This type in particular should acknowledge the texture of her hair as part of her entire outfit. Unlike her high-contrast Winter sisters, the Antique Winter looks best with gentle contrasts, colors that tend to meld and blend: rusty brick, gray green, and ash.

Fabulous Fabrics:
Brocade, cashmere knit, handkerchief linen, organdy.

Signature Scent:
Musk.

Must-Haves:
The Keeper of the Hearth will look stunning in a collarless bib-front blouse, riding-style jacket, trousers with a grommet and lace-up detail, an East Indian Jamawar shawl wrap skirt, or a chiffon late-1910s-inspired tea dress. Her romantic look needs some definition and clarity, so she needs to avoid any elements that might detract from her dreamy, Guinevere-like aura. The Antique Winter is blessed with a palette whose colors resemble that of an old map. She has a quiet beauty that doesn't require a lot of ornamentation, which is good, because she doesn't really enjoy making a fuss over herself. She may wear her hair cut short so she doesn't have to do much with it, and she rarely resorts to makeup.

Must-Avoids:
Primary colors and high-tech patterns—anything too modern, jarring, and high-contrast-y. Let this lady pass on high-tech athletic-inspired looks and 1950s perkiness. Athletic inspiration usually incorporates high-contrast techno fabrics that give the garments an almost superhero costume quality. I'm not suggesting that the Antique Winter cancel all further workouts, but she will feel more comfortable in terrycloth sweats in dusty pastels of her palette. As for 1950s perkiness, such as full circle skirts and capri trousers, these looks convey an energy that is too structured and has too animated a line for this mellow type.

Personality and Spirit:
The Antique Winter is the most rooted of all the types. A true Keeper of the Hearth, she seems to be surrounded by a sense of history that sustains her and everyone who knows her. This is the friend who knows your story and your history, and reminds you of them when you need to hear them the most. Her roots are deep and her feelings run deep, too. She is generous with both her stories and her memories, but she isn't outwardly warm. She does appreciate nostalgia, though, and even sentimentality: She might arrange her living room around Grandma's antique chest, for example, or build a wardrobe around a vintage dress that reminds her of Mom. On the other hand, she hates clutter, and since environments are very important to her, she may be ruthless in her efforts to streamline her home or office. Despite her love of home, the Keeper of the Hearth is actually quite fond of travel, though she's more of an anthropologist than your everyday tourist. She might be fascinated by the fertility rites of a lost tribe in Kenya, for example, or by the evolution of a grape in the Loire Valley.

She enjoys the human race and is unfailingly interested in our collective accomplishments and history. What better pastime for a Keeper of the Hearth, than to know all she can about where we all come from and where we might be going?

6. Playful Winter

Archetype:
The Ballerina.

Celebrity:
Victoria Beckham, Kate Beckinsale, Kelly Monaco, Winona Ryder.

Motto:
"Let's play make-believe."

Secret Superpower:
This playful creature has such a strong sense of fantasy that she can pull you into her dream world with her.

Kryptonite:
When our Ballerina flies free, she does so brilliantly. But when she tries to control her life or other people's, she might come crashing back to earth.

Nature Image:
Miniature roses, baby's breath.

Artists:
Victorian fairy painters; Sir Joshua Reynolds.

Charming Contrasts:
Medium contrast is best. Though this type is dramatic, she is also playful, which isn't supported by too harsh a contrast. I

strongly suggest outerwear in non-***Base*** colors for this Winter, for it lightens up the cold rainy day. A long wrap coat in her ***romantic*** color is the perfect way to lighten up a ***Second Base*** sweater dress and makes going out in the cold much more fun!

Fabulous Fabrics:
Tulle, stretch velvet, stretch wool gabardine, cotton sateen, Chantilly lace.

Signature Scent:
Lavender.

Must-Haves:
Our Playful Winter will look marvelous in her long double-breasted coat with peplum, as well as in her 1950s beaded cardigan, long tulle skirt, flamenco-style trousers, and 1920s-style flapper dress. She needs to find clothes that set off her playful, slightly theatrical nature. Nothing about the Ballerina is flashy or gimmicky. She looks best in clothes with simple, pretty lines, and as befits a Ballerina, she looks terrific in wrapped ballet sweaters, ballet flats, tights, and knits. I would encourage this type to try to play with proportion, such as a long coat over a short skirt and tights or finding a few more theatrical pieces to incorporate into her wardrobe, such as a velvet Victorian-styled coat, a cameo pin, or a blouse with a jabot detail. That will satisfy her need for flair while still keeping her clothed in the colors that are right for her.

Must-Avoids:
A man's-style barn jacket or anything that looks like a uniform—those styles are just too harsh and masculine for our Playful Winter's fun-loving, floaty personality. And this lighthearted dancer needs to avoid shoes with heavy soles that weigh her inner Ballerina down. Let the Ballerina pass as well

on short shorts and heavily padded shoulders. Her flirtatious
nature requires a somewhat free-spirited look, but very short
shorts or skirts will make her flirtation seem slightly crass. She
also doesn't need to look as though she's trying so hard; since
she gets lots of attention, she can chill a bit. Heavily padded
shoulders add too strong a silhouette for this type.

Personality and Spirit:

The Playful Winter is the most playful and light-handed of
all the Winter types. She's full of energy and ferocious about
any project to which she's devoted, though she usually prefers
to work on one project at a time. She's a bit theatrical, but
not in the grand manner, more like someone who enjoys
make-believe. No one is more fun to have at a party than
the Ballerina, whether she's the guest or the hostess. She'd
be more likely to invite friends to a restaurant than to her
home, but her blithe, generous nature makes the public place
feel comfortable, even intimate. Playful, gentle, and spirited,
she appears to float through life—but like the Ballerina she
resembles, her airy, effortless quality results from dedication,
hard work, and the courage to take intelligent risks.

Creating Your Authentic Style: Look for your Archetype
among the six choices under your Season. Identify the one that
seems to fit you best.

My Archetype: _____

UNDERSTANDING YOUR ARCHETYPE

Now that you've gotten acquainted with the twenty-four
Archetypes, I hope you've recognized not only yourself but
your loved ones, friends, and colleagues. I want you to follow

your **Archetype**—but I also want you to use it not as a strait-jacket but as a guide. If you have an article of clothing or a pair of shoes that "sound" wrong but feel right, I hope you'll trust your instincts. My ultimate goal is for you to develop your own **authentic style,** so that you'll put your own unique stamp on my advice.

I want you to follow my advice *most* of the time, however, especially at first. Sometimes, when we're used to one image of ourselves, it can be hard to open up to new possibilities, especially if we're at all anxious about revealing some aspect of ourselves—our sexuality, our authority and power, our play-ful, frivolous side. If you can, give at least one or two of my suggestions a real try, so you can see how it feels to show the world more of yourself. You may be pleasantly surprised at the results!

Meanwhile, you're now ready to move on from Showing Your True Colors to finding you some outfits that are Ready to Wear. Let's prepare for this transition by summing up every-thing you've learned in your **Authentic Style** Chart.

Creating Your Authentic Style: Keep track of the discoveries you've made so far by filling out the following chart:

MY TRUE COLORS

My *Essence* Color *(my version of white, the skin tone that harmonizes the colors of my palm)*: _____

My *Romantic* Color *(my version of red, the color that matches my face when I blush, my ears when they're cold, or a pinched fingertip)*: _____

My Dramatic Color *(my version of blue, taken from the most dominant color of the veins in my wrist):* _____

My Energy Color *(the darkest part of my iris, but not the ring around my iris):* _____

My Tranquil Color *(the lightest part of my iris):* _____

My First Base *(my version of black, the dark ring around my pupil):* _____

My Second Base *(my version of brown, the darkest color of my hair or eyebrows):* _____

My Third Base *(my version of khaki, the lightest color of my hair or eyebrows):* _____

My Authentic Style: _____

My Season: _____

My Archetype: _____

PART II:

ready to wear

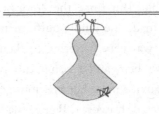

7

shades of emotion:

choosing colors and clothes for every occasion

one of my favorite clients was a Wisconsin woman named Renée, a retired nurse who came to know me when I did the palettes of her daughter, her best friend, and, eventually, her sister. Although Renée had actually had a color consultation twenty-five years previously, she had only been informed of her season—Summer—along with a few key colors that might look good on her. Her friends and family had convinced her that she might be able to get more detailed and empowering suggestions from someone who could help her find her **true colors** and her **authentic style,** and so she agreed to see me.

She showed up wearing a cute little cotton top in dark hyacinth, a lovely color that I immediately identified as Renée's **First Base,** her most formal neutral and her version of black. It was a blazing hot summer day, and she'd matched the top with some flattering shorts and a pair of sandals—a supercasual outfit, in other words, but one that jarred, to my eye, with the formal color of the *First Base.* On another woman, that dark hyacinth might have been a *dramatic* or an *energy* color, perfect for adding a touch of drama or some energy-balancing support to a casual ensemble. But since the color was Renée's *First Base,* it somehow made the whole outfit seem heavy.

Still, the color was very flattering to Renée's gray-brown skin and ash-brown hair, and I congratulated her on having gotten such good advice from her previous consultant. Instead of the smile I expected, however, Renée made a face.

"See," she said uncomfortably, "this was kind of a test. I know this is *supposed* to be a good color for me. But I don't know. I wore it on purpose because I never did think it made me 'pop' and I wondered if you would think so, too."

"Well," I said carefully, "it *is* a good color for you. But although that color might have quite different effects on other people, for you, it's your version of black. That means it's quite formal and not really the perfect choice for a casual little top-and-shorts outfit, any more than you'd want a suit jacket in a Hawaiian print. A suit is supposed to look serious, and a little cotton top is supposed to look fun and playful. So normally, you'd choose your *First Base* for your power suit and a more casual color for your T-shirt."

Renée was fascinated by the way that understanding her *true colors* helped her figure out not only what looked good on her but also how to use each color to its best effect. Later that year, when she stood up at her daughter's wedding, she did her bag and her shoes in her *First Base* dark hyacinth and it added just the touch of formality and grace that a huge wedding calls for. In understanding how to match each of her *true colors* to the correct occasion, Renée had truly understood The Color of Style.

The Power of Color

Now that you know your **true colors,** you're ready, like Renée, to start matching them to the correct occasion. Remember Camilla from Chapter 2, the therapist who had to switch her office from that **dramatic** shade of blueberry to her **essence** color of peach? Camilla had also learned that different types of colors affect us differently—and that we can learn to use those differences to our advantage.

Now that you know how to choose the colors, clothes, and objects that express your authentic self, it's time to start getting more specific about which parts of yourself to express when. That's what this chapter is all about. So if you'd like to start fine-tuning *your* use of color, read on.

Your True Colors

Essence **Color:** The color that harmonizes your skin tones and reveals your most genuine, open, and essential self; your version of *white;* wear it when you are having an intimate conversation, when you are meditating, or when you want to be completely open and honest.

Romantic **Color:** The color reflected by your flushed skin, which reveals your passion, your sexual energy, and your romantic self; your version of *red;* wear it on a hot date, a romantic evening, or any time you want your passion to show.

Dramatic **Color:** The color taken from the shade of your veins, which shows your power, your charisma, and your sense of authority; your version of *blue;* wear it on a job interview, for a formal presentation, or any time you want to make a strong impression.

Energy **Color:** The color seen in the darkest part of your iris (not the ring around your iris), which taps into the deepest sources of your energy; helps you restore and balance your energy; wear it when you want to be calm, self-possessed, and centered, such as at a family reunion, a meeting with your child's teacher, or a corporate retreat.

Tranquil **Color:** The color taken from the lightest part of your iris, which reveals the deepest sources of your tranquility; helps you relax and release stress; wear it when you want to recover from a challenging situation, such as after a long day at work.

First Base: The color found in the ring around your iris; your most formal and powerful neutral; your version of *black;* wear it for a formal occasion, such as an important meeting at work.

Second Base: The color taken from the darkest shade of your hair; a warmer and less formal neutral; your version of *brown;* wear it for a slightly less formal occasion, such as an ordinary day at work.

Third Base: The color seen in the lightest version of your hair; a playful and informal neutral; your version of *khaki;* wear it for a casual occasion, such as a beach party.

DATES AND ROMANCE

As we've seen, your romantic color is your version of red, the color that expresses your passion, your sexual energy, and your romantic self. This is one obvious choice to wear on a date or romantic evening, since you will look and feel empowered, vivacious, and very sexy in this color. A dress displaying your finest assets is best.

However, if you're not sure whether or not you're interested in your companion, your *romantic* color might not necessarily be your first choice. On some level, your version of red conveys your sexual interest and perhaps even your availability, which isn't necessarily the message you're ready to give. In fact, wearing your *romantic* color might even seem like an accidental come-on to someone that you decide you're not interested in seeing again.

If you're still testing the waters, why not try your *energy* color as an early dating outfit? Your *energy* color, as you recall, both supports and empowers you, so it's terrific for getting you through an evening that may have its ups and downs. Wonderful for any unknown circumstance, your *energy* color is a terrific fail-safe—in a flattering, clingy dress or in more relaxed but still sexy outfits, such as a low-cut top and comfortable slacks or jeans.

Must-Avoids: I would not recommend relying on any *base* color for a date, as you risk looking neutral at best, severe or withdrawn at worst. Remember, colors take different aspects of your personality and reveal them to the world, whereas your *bases* simply offer a neutral canvas behind which you can hide. That's not quite fair to the person you're dating, since that indicates that you aren't really participating or sharing. If in true sitcom style, your mother has set you up on a date that you really don't want, your neutrals are a way of saying, "I'm not really here"—but in that case, why not just wear a veil, or better yet, simply cancel?

At the other end of the spectrum, your *dramatic* color risks making the evening all about you. If you want to make a strong impression, go ahead with your *dramatic* color, but then be aware that you're giving the message that, in this relationship, you intend to be the star of the show, rather than a warm and loving partner.

Job Interviews and Business Appointments

For any situation in which your goal is to make a strong impression, your dramatic color is your best friend. On business occasions, you can use it as an accent, such as a dramatic-colored blouse with a First Base or Second Base suit. Or you might go for an even bigger splash by choosing a suit entirely in your dramatic color.

Your *dramatic* color is especially useful for situations in which you're competing for attention with lots of other people. For example, if you're interviewing for a job or a contract for which many other candidates are being seen, this color will make sure you're at your most visually memorable for your potential employer or client. This color shows you as a dynamic, powerful individual. You will notice when you wear it that it also has the ability to perk you up if you're feeling a bit tired. You are forced to match the energy of the color. If you have multiple interviews, I suggest repeating the color in a different form for each round—a suit one time, a blouse the second time, a dress the third time.

Must-Avoids: *Third Base* colors are supercasual and might convey that you're not taking this job seriously. Of course, it's always a good rule to dress for the position you're interviewing for, as though you were ready to start work as soon as the interview ended. But even if you're interviewing for a type of job that requires relatively informal work clothes, you still want to look dedicated, energetic, and as though you were prepared to make a serious commitment—whereas your relaxed *Third Base* "khaki" will give precisely the opposite impression.

By the same token, I'd suggest avoiding your "spa" *tranquil* color unless you're interviewing for a position in an actual spa.

The *tranquil* color is good for conveying a calm, laid-back aura, which might be useful for some jobs—therapist, school counselor, and day-care worker come to mind. Even so, you probably want your job interview to convey a more energetic impression than the relaxed *tranquil* color.

AN IMPORTANT MEETING

If you're attending an important meeting, I'd advise going with your First Base, probably in a suit, since this is your most formal color. If you know ahead that the meeting is very serious and you wish to appear open and neutral, I recommend a monochromatic suit or dress with a similar-colored jacket. If the meeting could go in many different directions and you want to try to influence it, show your passion and your power by incorporating your romantic or dramatic color into the ensemble, perhaps in a blouse or a shell under your suit jacket. As you might expect, the romantic color will help you to feel confident in your passion, your warmth, and your attractiveness. Your dramatic color puts people on notice that you intend to steamroll your agenda into the meeting, while giving you a little power boost as well.

Must-Avoids: Stay away from your *essence* color at a meeting like this. It makes you far too open and vulnerable.

A RELAXED MEETING

If you're attending a more relaxed meeting, go for a Second Base outfit—suit, slacks, or skirt—with a gently supporting energy- or tranquil-colored blouse. As we've seen, your Second Base "brown" is far less formal than your First Base "black," and the more relaxed choice should carry over into a less stressful meeting. If it's summer or one of those climates where it's always summer—Southern California, Hawaii, and the Gulf Coast region—you might even be able to get away with your least formal Third Base neutral.

A relaxed meeting means that you won't be faced with any wild cards or with any reasons to roll up your sleeves and spar. Since you won't have to prove yourself, your *energy* color is perfect: It supports you just the way you are but also energizes you to suggest new ideas or innovative approaches if you like. Your *tranquil* color will convey to others and yourself that if other people come up with great ideas, you won't stand in their way.

Must-Avoids: If you wear clothes in your *dramatic* or *romantic* colors, you may appear too powerful, if not too dominant. Somehow, these intense colors strike the wrong note at a relaxed meeting, a chord that's too high-pitched and that immediately sets up a kind of competition with others, especially other women. If you bring too much energy into the room by the colors that you wear, all of a sudden your relaxed meeting may not be relaxed anymore.

TRAVELING

When you're in for a long day on a plane, train, or automobile, you couldn't do better than to wear your energy color, the color that both energizes and relaxes you. No other color in your palette has such duality and ease, making it the perfect color to help you make the transition from catching a snooze on the flight to meeting your childhood friend at the airport gate. Your energy color will make you feel supported and safe during your nap and then energized enough to give your friend a big bear hug.

Must-Avoids: I'd advise against wearing a *First Base* color during your travels, since this more formal color will make it hard for you to relax. It's hard to sleep comfortably in a *First Base* color, or even to daydream, rest, or work productively. If you have to walk right off the plane and into a high-powered business meeting with no time to change, I'd suggest taking off the *First Base* suit jacket while you're traveling and wrapping yourself in a *tranquil*- or an *energy*-colored pashmina. You'll replenish your serenity and your energy while you're in transit, and then you can quickly don that *First Base* suit jacket before you disembark.

YOGA AND MEDITATION

If you're engaging in these serene activities at home, I suggest your essence color. What better way to get in touch with your essential self? Home is your sanctuary, and you're entitled to enjoy it in clothing that makes you feel entirely open and vulnerable.

If, on the other hand, you're meditating or doing yoga at a spa or health club, I suggest your *tranquil* color. It offers a little more psychic protection than your *essence* color, yet its serenity will still help you to harmonize your own energies with the reserves of peace and calm you're trying to access.

Must-Avoids: I wouldn't advise choosing a *romantic* or *dramatic* color for these peaceful activities, since both colors are likely to energize you. At the very least, choose lighter tints and less saturated versions of these colors: pale coral instead of the brighter, more intense version; light mint green rather than bright spearmint. The less intense colors will feel less stimulating and more relaxing.

EXERCISE

For high-energy exercise I suggest your romantic and dramatic colors, the two highest-energy colors on your palette. They will help you feel invigorated, alive, and energized while you are kickboxing, working the treadmill, or pumping some iron.

Must-Avoids: I'd stay away from your *essence* color. It will make you feel too naked and vulnerable, which may make it hard to gear up for an intense workout.

A FORMAL EVENT

Many people feel obligated to dress in black for a special occasion, especially if it calls for "black-tie." But I urge you to go for your own First Base "black" rather than a genuine black (unless, of course, your "black" is true black!). Depending on the formality of the event, a long or short dress or even a dressy suit in your First Base color is always right. Because your First Base is a form of black, you will feel at your most formal, and your "party manners" will blossom automatically.

Another option is to wear a *dramatic*-colored or *romantic*-colored outfit, highlighting your power or your passion. I'm all for making a grand entrance with a great splash of color, as long as you're aware that these colors will help make you more of a center of attention. Your *First Base,* on the other hand, will help you blend in while still looking glamorous and appropriate. So consider the nature of the event: Is it to honor someone else, your boss or your parents perhaps, or is it the type of party where you can network, look for romance, and otherwise allow yourself to shine? Your assessment of how much attention you want to draw to yourself can help you decide whether to go with a neutral or a color.

Must-Avoids: Your *Third Base* "khaki" will definitely be way too casual for a formal event, even if you dress it up with a *dramatic*-colored scarf or some sparkly jewelry. Unless the formal event is being held in the tropics or in a very casual environment, I'd avoid this route.

THE BEACH

For chilling at the beach, you'll obviously want to choose your least formal color, and by now you know that is your Third Base, the most casual color in your palette: light, relaxed, and carefree. I suggest pairing it with your essence color and with paler, pastel versions of your romantic, dramatic, energy, and tranquil colors, depending on whether you want to look sexy, powerful, energized, or super-relaxed and calm.

Must-Avoids: Although when lounging by a swimming pool, you might want a glamorous *First Base* bathing suit or a sexy *romantic*-colored suit, both of these colors take more energy to wear than your *Third Base.* Save these high-energy suits for more demanding occasions and kick back with your *Third Base* at the beach.

COMFORTING A FRIEND

In a time when you need to offer empathy and support, your tranquil color is the perfect choice: It allows you to remain present with your friend while staying mellow, and your energy won't take any focus from your friend in her time of need. If you choose a soft, tactile garment, made of suede, fleece, or cashmere, your presence will be even softer and more comforting.

Must-Avoids: I wouldn't suggest wearing a *First Base* color on "a mission of mercy"; it's too severe and in some ways, too funereal. Save the *First Base* for a more formal occasion where your goal is less to offer comfort than to blend in with the crowd.

A Funeral

As we've seen, your First Base is your version of black, a traditional Western color for funerals. It allows you to preserve a kind of formality that enables a room full of grieving people to keep it together while still conveying your sorrow and regret. While in private, your friend may need a gentle comfort that allows her to break down and grieve; at a public occasion for mourning, she will appreciate your helping her to maintain some boundaries.

Must-Avoids: In Western cultures, at least, stay away from *romantic*-colored garments. It looks as though you're celebrating your own vitality at an occasion intended to mark a loved one's death.

Family Occasions

Your energy color is so perfect for family occasions that if it didn't already exist, it would have had to be invented, just to give you some much-needed nurturing and support for what are often stressful (if rewarding) events. Your energy color allows you to feel nurtured while offering your own nurturing—and what could be a better way to show up at a family event than that?

If you're lucky enough to be able to really let down your guard with your family, go ahead and wear your *tranquil* color. Otherwise, stick to your supportive *energy* color—and be glad it works so well!

Must-Avoids: For your own peace of mind as well as everyone else's, do not wear *dramatic* or *romantic* colors to family occasions: These colors are simply too powerful. With family, the emotional connections run so deep that you don't need the more overt signals necessary in other relationships. Rather, you need to be subtle, almost subliminal, because your histories and connections supersede the here and now.

I would also suggest avoiding all your *Bases,* because, honestly, you need some color to support you. If you do wear *Bases,* make sure you brighten them up with your *energy* and perhaps also your *tranquil* color to support you.

GUEST OF HONOR

If there was ever a time when you'd want to gracefully accept being the center of attention, it would be at an occasion where you're the guest of honor or otherwise a key person at the event: the choreographer at the opening night of a dance concert; the author at a book party; the candidate at a political event. Celebrate your distinctive self with your dramatic color or your romantic color, depending on whether you want to focus on your power or your passion.

Must-Avoids: If you stick to your neutrals by wearing your *Bases,* you're basically withholding yourself. And why would you refuse to share yourself with the people who have come together to celebrate you?

Holidays, Art Openings, and Other Special Occasions

If you're giving or attending a holiday party, you might choose the colors traditionally appropriate to the celebration—but your version of those colors. At a Christmas party, for example, my version of red and green would be tangerine and olive, so I'd wear those colors for a very personal interpretation of Yuletide cheer. I also tend to choose something more theatrical or costume-y when I'm the holiday host, something from another period or culture, or an item that is ethnic or vintage in some way. You might want to do the same, or at least choose a unique garment or some kind of striking accessory.

For holiday parties at home, I'd otherwise recommend your *romantic* color, evoking the warmth and love to be found at your hearth. For public fetes, consider your *dramatic* color, or some combination of both *romantic* and *dramatic*. These are your most striking colors, so make the most of them!

Must-Avoids: *Please* don't let yourself be bulldozed into wearing colors that don't work for you, traditional or not. You can find some way of making the traditions your own while still choosing the colors, clothes, and objects that express your authentic self.

Your Wedding

Here's another case in which sticking strictly with tradition may not be quite right for you, since the traditional pure white wedding dress is very unlikely to be right for most people. And if you are really committed to your true colors and your authentic style, pure white may seem far too anonymous and not nearly personal enough.

Your *essence* color, however—your version of white—is a more unexpected and often far more beautiful choice for a bridal gown. It conveys that on your special day, you are feeling light and easy, ready to embark on a new journey. Wearing your *essence* color will make you feel natural, completely whole, yet vulnerable—and your glow will be your most lovely.

An alternative is to find another version of your white by matching the color of your gown to the "white" of your eye. You will still look innocent and pure—and beautiful.

Finally, like Alys from Chapter 3, you can choose your *tranquil* color for an extra dose of serenity on your wedding day. You will appear relaxed and glowing, and you may be grateful for the additional reserves of calm.

Must-Avoids: Please don't wear pure white unless that is the color of the white of your eye. If pure white isn't one of your colors, it won't make you look pure but rather sallow, flushed, or blotchy. Why give up your chance to be the most beautiful bride ever?

Creating Your Authentic Style: Fill in the chart below so you know which of your true colors to wear for which occasions. If you like, name types of garments—suit, dress, slacks, bathing suit—as well as colors.

OCCASION	TRUE COLOR OPTIONS	GARMENTS
Dates and Romance	My *Romantic* Color: My *Energy* Color:	

Occasion	True Color Options	Garments
Job Interviews and Business Appointments	My *First* Base: My *Second* Base: My *Dramatic* Color:	
An Important Meeting	My *First* Base: My *Romantic* Color: My *Dramatic* Color:	
A Relaxed Meeting	My *Second* Base: My *Third* Base: My *Energy* Color: My *Tranquil* Color:	
Traveling	My *Energy* Color: My *Tranquil* Color:	
Yoga and Meditation At Home **Outside the Home**	My *Essence* Color: My *Tranquil* Color:	

Occasion	True Color Options	Garments
Exercise	My *Romantic* Color: My *Dramatic* Color:	
A Formal Event	My *First* Base: My *Romantic* Color: My *Dramatic* Color:	
The Beach	My *Third* Base: My *Essence* Color: My *Romantic* Color, Pastel Version: My *Dramatic* Color, Pastel Version: My *Essence* Color, Pastel Version: My *Tranquil* Color, Pastel Version:	
Comforting a Friend	My *Tranquil* Color:	
A Funeral	My *First* Base:	

OCCASION	TRUE COLOR OPTIONS	GARMENTS
Family Occasions	My *Energy* Color: My *Tranquil* Color:	
Guest of Honor	My *Romantic* Color: My *Dramatic* Color:	
Holidays, Art Openings, and Other Special Occasions **At Home** **Outside the Home**	My Version of *Holiday* Colors: My *Romantic* Color: My *Dramatic* Color:	
My Wedding	My *Essence* Color: The *White* of My Eye: My *Tranquil* Color:	

8

re-creating your closet:

deciding what to keep and what to let go

I once worked with a woman in Florida whose sense of style was very strong. Even before she met me, Lila had a good sense of her *true colors* and her **authentic style.** She took to my additional suggestions with enthusiasm, purchasing lovely new garments that were right for her while pruning out of her closet the few that weren't.

Or so I thought. Then Lila asked me to her home to work with her on her closet, and I saw a number of garments that, frankly, didn't work at all. A Dynamic Winter, Lila looked best in colors such as teal, silver, and fuchsia, and her **Base** colors were charcoal gray, aubergine, and oyster. Why, then, did I see in her closet a tomato red dress, a cobalt blue blouse, and a beige skirt-and-sweater set?

I mentioned the garments as tactfully as I could, but to my surprise, Lila was nodding vigorously. "Oh, I know, they're all wrong," she said even before I could finish my sentence. "I'll never be able to wear them—that's obvious."

I wanted to ask her why she had them, then, but again she beat me to the punch. "My husband gave them to me for my birthday," she explained. "He was so sweet about it, too. He said, 'I thought these would look nice on you,' so of course, what could I say? He had never bought me clothes before, and I didn't want to hurt his feelings. So when we went out to dinner for my birthday, I wore that skirt and sweater, but honestly, I never felt right in them. I put on a little bit more makeup than usual, I spent more time on my hair, I even wore a little more jewelry than I normally do, but nothing could ever make those colors feel right."

Lila could see how curious I was, so she went on with her story. It turned out that her husband's brother had recently gotten a pilot's license so he could fly a small plane, and Lila's husband had decided that he might like to do that, too. Lo and behold, the license test revealed that he was severely color-blind, unable to tell red from green. No wonder he hadn't been able to pick out clothes for Lila!

"After he found out," Lila went on, "he was quite embarrassed about the clothes. He said, 'Oh, I bet they don't look good on you at all, do they?' What could I say? If I throw them out now, it will seem as though I'm reinforcing the idea that he's handicapped, that there's something important to me that he can't do. No clothes are worth making him feel that way."

I admired Lila's loyalty and devotion—and I admired even more her sense of tact. Because eventually she did get rid of the unwearable clothes, sending them to a local thrift shop that supported worthy causes by selling high-end "gently worn" clothes at affordable prices. When her husband asked, she said casually, "You know, I had them at one end of my closet, and that's where the leak was, remember? I sent them to the dry cleaner's immediately, but they never could get the stains out."

Now, why am I telling you this story? Because if Lila could eventually get rid of *her* "below-grade" garments, despite their emotional history and importance to her marriage, *so can you.*

Believe me, I *know* how hard it is to let go of clothing that doesn't work. But if you're really committed to using your clothes, colors, and objects to express your authentic self, you *have* to respect your closet. Don't worry, I'll help!

So let's get started. In this chapter, I'll do for you what I do for all my clients: show you how to go through your closet and figure out which items to keep and which to let go. In later chapters, we'll see how you can make the most of the clothes you have while being as efficient and economical as possible in buying the new things you need to complete your look. But right now, the rewards for all your hard work are within your reach. So let's take the first step: re-creating your closet.

Overcoming "Closet Despair"

Make some time when you can focus totally on your closet—no phone, TV, or interruptions, and not even any music, so that nothing but your clothes can set the emotional tone. Ready? Open your closet door and take a good look. Do you see colors, clothes, and accessories that express your authentic self, clothes that can see you through your work, home life, social life, and the special events that brighten your days? Or do you see lots of garments that you now understand simply aren't right? If you're like most of my clients—a list that includes many high-fashion, high-profile, and stylish women—you may be looking at your closet in despair, wondering how so many unflattering pieces ended up in there.

Whether or not you're now happy with your current wardrobe, I don't want you to feel that you did anything wrong in
the past. There's a reason for everything in that closet. Maybe
your mother told you navy was appropriate, so you've got lots
of navy pieces, even though you now realize that it isn't one
of your *true colors.* Perhaps you've heard that all women need
a little black dress or a crisp white blouse or a red power suit,
and you thought you'd give it a try, though you now understand that these looks don't suit your *Archetype.* Maybe you've
been relying on a friend's advice, or a saleswoman's, or on what
the fashion magazines and retailers have chosen to feature that
season.

If you are feeling "closet despair," please, don't beat yourself
up! The good news is that now you're getting in touch with
who you really are and which types of clothing express your
authentic self. So take a deep breath and let's start going through
that closet, keeping what's right and letting go of what's not.

Now, if you've got access to a hefty clothing budget, lots of
time, and a burst of energy, you may decide you want to do it
all at once—throw out everything that isn't absolutely perfect
and then run right out and start over. If you're that type of
all-or-nothing woman, more power to you! But if, like many
of us, you find such rapid change rather daunting—and especially if, like many of us, you're living on a budget!—here's a
step-by-step approach that offers a slow, steady, and affordable
way to reach your goal.

Step One:
Identify the Hits—and the Near Hits

Maybe you'll have one fabulous garment that fits your true
persona. Or maybe you'll have three, or six, or none. Start by

putting those "A-plus" garments on the left side of your closet. Our ultimate goal is that everything in your closet should be A-plus, and we won't settle for anything less! But we're going to get there little by little, in a steady affordable way, so don't throw everything away quite yet. After all, you can't be naked all of the time!

Once you've found the garments that are perfect—the colors, clothes, and accessories that express your authentic self—look for the near perfect. Maybe your *true colors* include a deep olive and you have some trousers that are dark sage. Before, you might not even have registered the difference in these two shades of green; now, thanks to the work you've done training your eye and refining your sense of style, you can see that these pants are not *quite* right. Meanwhile, though, they're close enough. Sometime, when you have the time and money to go shopping again, you'll find yourself a new pair. Until then, put these pants in the middle of your closet.

Continue with this process—perfect clothes to the left; near perfect to the center—until you've worked your way through your entire closet. Push all the hits and near hits a little farther to the left, so you can look at them as a group. Take a moment to appreciate how all of the colors relate to one another and tell the story of who you are. As my client Faith Prince said years ago, they create a visual map of your personality—take some time to enjoy that map.

Take another moment to ask yourself what statement these clothes make about you. There on the hangers you should be able to read, "I'm playful, I'm fun!" or "I'm striking and dramatic." Maybe you'll read, "I'm passionate and serious—but I have a quirky sense of humor," or "I'm cheerful one moment and dreamy the next," or "I'm so full of contradictions, you can't pin me down to *anything*." One way or another, the clothes that are right for you will express who you are, illustrating your "character," as if you were starring in a play or a film. Taking that process of self-expression further and further is now your goal.

Step Two:
Try Wearing Only the "Right" Clothes

For a week or so before you go shopping, try dressing yourself only from the left side of the closet. Wear only the hits and the near hits, and accessorize them with only the hits and near hits among your shoes, scarves, belts, bags, and jewelry. You may have to repeat some outfits more than you'd like, but the experience of being faithful to your true colors and your authentic style should be worth the temporary limitations. (You can read on to the next chapter for some specific suggestions about how to get every garment to do double, triple, and even quadruple duty, making the most of every part of your wardrobe.)

So, what happens when you start to dress like who you really are? Do you get more compliments? A different type of romantic attention? More respect at work? Do you feel more confident? Sexier? Calmer? More comfortable? If you like, keep a journal for that week to help you focus on your experience. Or just pay attention to the effect that embracing your **authentic style** has on your experience with others and with yourself.

Step Three:
Let Go of Whatever Doesn't Suit You

If you're one of those lucky people who finds it easy to get rid of clothes that don't work for you, I salute you! Bundle up those "not right" clothes and give the still-wearable garments to a friend or a thrift shop. Those stained, stretched-out, and worn-out articles can go right into the garbage—nobody's going to wear them.

If you're like most of us, though, you may not find it so easy to let go of the wrong garments. Here are some suggestions for letting go of items that do not suit your **true colors** or reflect your **authentic style,** along with clothes that just don't fit anymore and garments that are worn out, stained, or hopelessly out of style.

- *Remember that the garments in your wardrobe have three types of value: monetary value, emotional value, and use value.* The price you paid for a garment may reflect its monetary value. The emotional associations with an item are what create its emotional value. Both types of value can lead us to hold on to clothes that either don't work for us anymore or never worked for us in the first place: clothes that have no use value.

  Many of my clients tell me they can't let go of a high-end blouse or a designer gown "because I paid so much for it." But if the garment doesn't make you look and feel fabulous, what good is it to you, really? Maybe spending all that money on it was the right decision at the time, or maybe it wasn't; either way, you're not getting any use value out of letting the expensive item hang in your closet, and you're actually creating negative use value by wearing it when it doesn't suit you. Take a deep breath, hope that the next owner of the garment has better luck, and pass it on.

- ***Don't turn your closet into a clothing museum.***
Many of us hold on to garments for historical
reasons: that bright-red T-shirt commemorating
our high-school graduation; that silky sweater
we wore to our engagement dinner; the jeans we
wore to the carnival on our first date with our
soul mate. I'm not saying you should give these
clothes to a thrift shop if they make your heart beat
faster—but please, please, please, *don't* leave them in
your closet! Create a memory box or find a storage
closet with an extra shelf and store your memory
clothing somewhere out of sight, the way you keep
other kinds of souvenirs. It's important that your
closet feel full of items that you could wear that
day, so that you feel energized every time you open
the closet door. More important, you want your
closet to reflect your true self, just as you want
every outfit to do so. If a "historical" item doesn't
do that, put it somewhere else so it doesn't disrupt
the energy of your everyday closet.

- ***Get rid of things you bought for convenience.*** Okay,
so one day, you were out in the middle of a field
at the county antiques show and it started to rain.
You looked around for something to wear, and the
only thing you could find was a fluorescent lilac
poncho that a local vendor was selling. I'm glad
you were able to stay warm and dry that day—but
if the look and style are wrong for you now, you
don't have to keep the poncho! Put its price down
as part of the cost of that otherwise lovely albeit
rainy day, and let it go.

- *Share the "extras" with your friends.* If you've got friends who are also reading this book or who just want to refresh their own wardrobes, you could always organize a swap. See if their won't-work clothes are right for you even as you offer to share your own not-right garments with them. Throw a luncheon and have everyone come with a big bag of clothes she no longer wants. Try things on for one another and then bundle up the un-chosen for the thrift shop.

- *If you've decided a garment isn't right for you, you really aren't going to wear it again anyway. Ever.* In the twenty years I've been working with clients, I've never seen a single exception. Anything they've begged me to let them keep ("I love that designer, and I paid a fortune for his latest skirt!") just sits on a shelf, unworn, while they revel in their "hits," "near hits," and eventually, their new purchases. My clients have gotten rid of every single one of those wrong-but-I-can't-let-it-go pieces within a few months of our first shopping trip. Give yourself that transitional time if you must—but the sooner you let the wrong garment go, the sooner a right one can come in to take its place.

- *If you don't free yourself of the old, you won't have room for the new.* Have you ever noticed that sometimes, new things can't come into our lives until the old ones are on the way out? A woman in an "okay" relationship doesn't really redefine what kind of partner she wants until her boyfriend has called it quits—freeing her to find a new guy who makes her much happier. An advertising exec who's frustrated with the lack of purpose in her life doesn't think about finding something more meaningful until there's talk of layoffs. And a woman with a closet full of old, worn-out, or not-quite-right clothes may never get the fabulous wardrobe she deserves until she's bundled up the B-minuses to make room for the A-pluses!

• *Know what you can and can't fix.* If a garment is the right color but somehow just seems wrong for your *Archetype,* you may be able to alter its tone or style with the right accessories or companion garment. A rather plain sweater in your *Second Base* might be enlivened with some high-contrast jewelry or with a scarf in a slightly lighter shade of the same color. A too-much tank patterned with splashy flowers and embroidered with sparkling beads could perhaps be "brought down" by wearing it under a *tranquil*-colored cardigan or a quiet *First Base* jacket. Look at the "Charming Contrast" suggestions in your *Archetype* in Chapter 6 and read on to my other suggestions for stretching your wardrobe in Chapter 9 to learn more about what to fix and what to let go.

Tips for Trying On

Having trouble evaluating your wardrobe? Here are some tips for assessing your garments as you try them on.

1. **Don't look at the garment—look at *you* in the garment.** You don't care, ultimately, about giving the

designer publicity—you care about how terrific you look. And remember, there's no such thing as a pretty color or an ugly color, only colors that look pretty or ugly *on you.*

2. **Ask yourself what the garment says about you.** If you were to walk into a room wearing this garment, how would people describe you? "Businesswoman"? "Open-minded"? "Artistic"? "Chic girl who just flew in from Europe"? "Biker chick"? "Liberal"? "Conservative"? Figure out that word and then hold it up to what you know about your personality, along with what you've learned in this book about your type. Does the word that fits your outfit also fit you?

3. **If you have to think too long, the garment needs to go.** Anything that looks great on you should be obviously great, an instant "wow." If you can't see the "wow" right away, the item isn't helping you to show your *true colors* or your *authentic style.* Do what Lila did, and let those below-grade garments go!

SHOULD I KEEP IT OR LET IT GO?

Still having trouble releasing those not-quite-right outfits? Here is one more checklist you can use as you try them on:

1. *How long has it been since I've worn it?* More than a year? It's history. After all, you've had 365 opportunities to choose this article of clothing. If you haven't taken even one of them, there's probably a good reason.

2. **Is it really an A-plus?** Most of us spend far too many years settling for B or even B-minus. I want your closet to be crammed with A-pluses, and A-pluses only. So if a garment doesn't make the grade, it's gone. If you still aren't sure, ask yourself, "Did I smile when I put this on?" You know what to do if you didn't. . . .

3. **Does it still fit?** Maybe you've been working out more and a garment that once fit beautifully is now grabbing you in the wrong places. Maybe you're more active now—your infant has grown into a toddler and you spend a lot more time running around after her. Or maybe, yes, you might have gained weight. The reason doesn't matter—the fit does. Only perfectly fitting garments belong in your closet.

4. **Is it still in good shape?** If your garment is stretched out, stained, or otherwise distressed, you don't want to be wearing it, no matter how beautiful it looked when you first bought it. Remember, its ultimate value isn't based on what you paid for it but on its current use to you. If you paid one hundred dollars at a local boutique for your favorite skirt and four dollars at a garage sale for your favorite shirt, as long as they're both your favorites, they have the same use value. To determine your garment's condition, ask yourself:
   - Are the cuffs frayed?
   - Are the elbows worn?
   - Is the waistband stretched?
   - Is the neck no longer pristine?

- Are the shoulders pilling?
- Is the whole garment still the right length, and if not, can you let the hem down?
- If the garment *can* be fixed, do you want to invest in fixing it? If not, let it go. And if it *can't* be fixed . . . well, like I said . . . You know what to do.

5. ***Does it duplicate something I have a better version of?*** Many of us find ourselves repeatedly buying the same thing because we know that it works for us and we feel good wearing it. That's all well and good, but we often don't get the best possible version of our "duplicate" garment. Do you really need two pencil skirts in the same color? Because I guarantee that you wear one of them more than the other. Let the second-best skirt go to the thrift shop or to a friend so you have room in your closet for a new skirt, maybe in a new color or a different style. There are so many lovely shades and silhouettes— why settle for just one?

6. ***Does it make you look like the person you really are?*** Many of my clients have gone out and bought items that they think they need—but that don't fit their true selves. Lainie, for example, was a free-spirited bohemian who earned most of her living selling her sketches and watercolors but who occasionally did some work for an advertising agency in Midtown Manhattan. She had bought a corporate-looking blazer for her forays into the business world, but it never really looked right on her. When we worked together, I helped her pick out a cute little embroidered jacket that looked as though she knew how

to dress while visiting the business world but also
revealed that she didn't live in it.

7. *Is it a costume you need—and will wear?* It's not as
though Lainie didn't need *something* to wear to her
midtown gigs. Likewise, my client Veronica liked to
have one superglamorous outfit on tap for the New
Year's Eve party she went to every year. It's fine to
have a costume in reserve as long as you really will
wear it and feel like yourself in it. Just make sure
that the costumes you're saving really do work for
you—and that you will either find or make an occasion to wear them!

The Stories We Tell Ourselves . . .

Do any of the following sentences sound familiar? They're
the stories we tell ourselves about why we should hold on to an
item of clothing that doesn't fit, is stained or stretched, or simply
isn't right for us. I promise you, *none* of them is sufficient reason
to hold on to a garment that doesn't make you look and feel
fabulous *right this very minute*!

Maybe I'll Lose Weight

Great. Then you can buy some new clothes that fit the new
you. They will be the perfect reward for reaching this goal.
Meanwhile, keeping a too-small item in your closet is just
a way to make yourself feel bad about how you look now.
Worse, it suggests that your real life is going to start later,
after the weight loss, instead of reminding you of the truth:
You get to look and feel fabulous, right this very minute, no
matter what you weigh.

Maybe It Will Come Back into Style

Speaking as a designer, I promise you: never gonna happen. Even when styles do get revived, retro looks aren't the same as actual vintage pieces. There's always a little modern twist on that fifties-style shirtdress or eighties-era power suit. If you absolutely love a garment and are one of those people who can pull off wearing vintage, feel free to wear something that seems out of style. But if you've been saving it for some future style revolution, stop living in the past or the future and let it go.

I Paid a Lot of Money for It

Unless your favorite accessory is an enormous price tag hanging in the center of your chest, this reason says nothing about how your garment looks on you, or about how it makes you feel. Maybe you feel glad about spending the money, or perhaps you feel regret—but either way, an expensive garment that doesn't flatter you and express your true self is like a gourmet meal that you're allergic to. Yes, it cost a lot of money—but it isn't going to make you feel good. Let it go to make room for something that does.

Someone I Love Gave It to Me

Does your loved one want you to wear something that isn't right for you? If so, consider putting the garment aside and wearing it when your loved one visits. If not, let it go so that someone else can benefit from your loved one's generosity.

I Wore It on a Special Occasion

Again, if looking at this special garment brings back a flood of memories, put it in a memory box. Or give it to the thrift store so someone else can create memories in it.

Either way, it doesn't belong in your working closet unless it looks great on you now.

I Love One Detail About It

It may be that the detail you love—the glowing opalescent buttons or the kicky beaded fringe at the hem—is just perfect for your **Archetype.** It's still not enough to redeem the whole garment, especially if the garment doesn't fit properly or is stained, stretched-out, or worn out. Even if the garment is in mint condition, however, one detail isn't enough to compensate for the color being incorrect. Promise yourself to keep looking for another item of clothing that has a similar detail—and let this piece go.

I Love the Idea of It

Often we love clothing that might look good on other people but that fits only an idea of ourselves. A long, flowing skirt suggests elegance and glamour—but doesn't flatter our figure. A crisp trench coat evokes mystery and intrigue—but doesn't suit our **Archetype.** If there's a garment whose idea you love but that doesn't make you look and feel great, find some other way to get those qualities into your life and your wardrobe, and let the garment go.

It's Perfectly Good—
There's Still a Lot of Wear in It

As someone who loves both quality and value, I appreciate the waste-not-want-not ethic. But keeping a garment that doesn't make you look and feel your best is the perfect definition of a false economy. You don't really gain anything—and you lose a great deal. A client once shared with me that Weight Watchers has a slogan about not feeling the need to eat everything on your plate: "You are not a garbage can." By the same token, you are not a thrift shop, and your closet is not a clothing museum. Get those gently used clothes over to a deserving group like Dress for Success (which helps women entering the job market dress appropriately) or to a high-end thrift shop that will share them with people who really need good clothes and can't afford them, and save your pennies to buy a garment that truly expresses you.

It Should Look Good on Me

As many stories throughout this book have made clear, we often find it baffling when a garment that should look good, doesn't. After reading this book, you may be able to identify what's wrong with an apparently perfect garment—or you may not. Either way, if something isn't making you look A-plus, let it go, whether or not you can explain why.

RESPECT YOUR CLOSET

Now that you've pared down your wardrobe to only your favorite items, you're almost ready to go shopping. But before you go out and fill in all those empty spaces in your closet, let's give your closet itself a little bit more attention.

Your goal ultimately is to open your closet door and be greeted by the sight of colors, clothes, and objects that express your true self. *Wow,* you find yourself thinking. *That's* me *hanging there—and there and there and there and there!* Every single hanger, every pair of shoes underneath, every scarf and hat and belt should reflect your own unique *authentic style.*

You want your closet to become a kind of shrine to yourself, a private space that supports and nurtures you. So make sure this

key area in your home is doing its job. If you possibly can, store the
vacuum cleaner somewhere else and find another place to keep
those old tax returns and the kids' castoff toys. Don't let your closet
become your *Picture of Dorian Gray,* the dirty little secret behind
your put-together look. Instead, let this be a well-cared-for space
that reflects your commitment to looking and feeling fabulous.

Express your commitment in a concrete way. Make sure
that your clothes are hung up properly. If you have a stretchy
jersey dress, drape it over two hangers—shoulders on one, waist
on another—so it doesn't stretch out. If you have some delicate
garments, invest in a few padded hangers to make sure they
keep their shape. And hang a full-length mirror in an easily
accessible place so you can see yourself as the world sees you,
not just from the shoulders up, but head to toe.

REVIEWING YOUR ACCESSORIES

Just as you've reviewed your closet to make sure every garment
in it is up-to-date, fits well, and looks great on you, so must you
do the same with your accessories. Every shoe, scarf, belt, hat,
and piece of jewelry needs to be sorted through, perhaps tried
on, certainly put into either a yes or a no pile.

Remember how your closet is not supposed to be a clothing museum? Well, your jewelry box is not supposed to be a
memory box, either. If you've got a concert button from twenty
years ago to remind you of your first rock concert or the night
your college boyfriend kissed you, put it into a special container
with the rest of your keepsakes. Your jewelry should be stored
or displayed in a convenient part of your bedroom or dressing
room. Including items that you'll never choose to wear is just
going to make it harder to choose the best possible accessories,
every single day.

Getting the Full View

If you're going to be reviewing most of your wardrobe, create a temporary three-way mirror. Arrange two full-length mirrors—perhaps the one from your closet door and the one in your bathroom—so that you can see both the front and the back view.

CARING FOR YOUR CLOSET

My client Letitia was a Dallas architect whose closet seemed to have a split personality. When she went through the process I've suggested for you—moving the clothes that were correct for her to the left and leaving the ones that were not to the right—her closet was split almost exactly down the middle. Half of the clothes really suited her perfectly, while the other half were just slightly off: a fuchsia blouse instead of her own magenta; a black plum evening gown instead of her true dramatic royal purple.

When I pointed this out, Letitia laughed, almost embarrassed. "The ones on the left were with my *first* personal shopper," she explained. "That woman really understood me, and everything she suggested suited me to a tee.

"Then she got pregnant and took some time off. The man who replaced her just didn't get me the same way. He suggested a lot of things that I now see are *almost* right—but I understand it now: 'Almost' is not good enough!"

Even though Letitia had bought the clothes the shopper had suggested, she hadn't actually worn them. Most of them had the tags still on—which was lucky, because now she wanted to return them all!

Letitia's story reminds me how important it is to respect your closet. With half of the garments inside it basically off-limits, Letitia found it demoralizing even to open her closet door. When she got rid of the inappropriate garments, she immediately felt better about getting dressed every morning. She had learned that the closet was an active, dynamic part of her life, and if she didn't keep it in good condition, she wasn't respecting herself. It was as though she had to draft the floor plan of a new building without her usual drafting table, working on an oversized book propped up on her lap. She couldn't work well without a drafting table, and she couldn't dress well without a well-organized closet. Neither can you.

Creating Your Authentic Style: Look at your newly organized closet and make two lists on the following chart: 1. **Clothes I Have** and 2. **Clothes I Need.** Use the second list as the basis for your work "revising" outfits in Chapter 9 and then to help you put together a shopping list for Chapter 10.

CLOTHES I HAVE

	GARMENT	COLOR
1.	_____	_____
2.	_____	_____
3.	_____	_____
4.	_____	_____
5.	_____	_____

CLOTHES I NEED

	GARMENT	COLOR
1.		
2.		
3.		
4.		
5.		

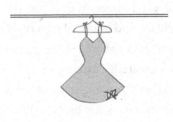

9

transforming your wardrobe:

turning so-so outfits into wows, making every outfit go further, and figuring out what to buy

I once did a series of makeovers on a television talk show, helping "ordinary" women see how they could transform their look on a budget. Although I love working with performers and celebrities, I enjoy even more seeing how creating an **authentic style** empowers every woman to claim her own personal beauty.

After the makeovers were complete and we were ready to resume taping, I happened to run into one of the women as we waited together in the greenroom. I thought she looked fantastic—and more important, *she* thought she looked fantastic. When I complimented her, though, she sighed.

"Yeah," she said, "I know, I look great. And I'm thrilled that I get to keep this one outfit after the taping is over. But this is it—my only great outfit! I'll never be able to do anything like this at home! And to be honest, I can't afford to buy anything else, not for quite a while."

She gestured to the clothes we had selected for her—a simple off white **Third Base** blouse over a fitted pair of **Second Base** dove gray thin-wale corduroy pants, worn with a textured **First Base** charcoal-plaid blazer. We'd filled out the look with a simple pewter necklace and a pair of silvery-gray earrings. The neutrals—off white, charcoal, and dove gray—dressed up with the metallic jewelry created a striking look.

"Actually," I told her, "you've got lots of options." I pointed out that she could wear this very same outfit with a different jacket—maybe a dark red or a deep green. "Even if the color isn't perfect," I told her, "you may be able to make do until you can afford another one, and meanwhile, you do have another outfit." Or she could wear the ensemble without the jacket, slipping a fitted tank top under the blouse and wearing the blouse tied at the waist instead of belted. Yet another option was to substitute a skirt for the pants, possibly with tall boots to make the look even more different.

"Eventually," I told her, "you can add more items, one garment at a time. Meanwhile, this outfit gives you a great place to start."

My TV client was thrilled with these new possibilities—and I hope you will be, too. Let's take a look at the B-plus and B-minus garments that *you* need to "restyle" while waiting for the time and/or money to buy new ones.

SUITS AND JACKETS

Fixing a So-so Garment

If you've got a neutral suit or jacket in a color that isn't one of your neutrals—say, a dark brown suit instead of your own First Base charcoal gray or your ideal Second Base caramel—get one solid blouse or shell in your essence color and another in your romantic color. These items will bring out your true colors via your skin tones and your blush tones, helping you to rise above the unfortunate neutral and providing some true tones for the eye to focus on.

Don't try to find items that will somehow magically turn the wrong neutral into the right one, creating a harmony that isn't there. Instead, ignore the incorrect neutral and just buy the right blouse, perhaps adding a scarf or some jewelry that brings out the *essence* or *romantic* color even more. Then, too, when you switch to the neutral suit or jacket that *is* right for you, you'll already have the garments to go with it.

In this situation, I would suggest avoiding a ***dramatic***-colored blouse or shell. Remember that both the *essence* and the *romantic* colors are based on your skin, whether your "regular" or your "flushed" skin tones. Your *dramatic* color, however, is based on your veins and is meant to provide the strongest possible "dramatic" contrast to your skin tones. With one of your own ***Base*** colors, a *dramatic* blouse or shell is terrific, but if your "wrong" suit or jacket is already not supporting your coloring, adding a *dramatic* note will just create more noise. Wait till you have one of your own true colors before bringing in a *dramatic* element.

Likewise, with a correct ***Base*** suit or jacket, you can happily wear an ***energy***-colored or ***tranquil***-colored blouse or shell. But if your ***Base*** color is wrong, these calm colors won't bring enough energy to the mix to counteract the problem. Again, wait till your ***Base*** color is right before adding them.

Making Every Garment Go Further

If you've got a terrific suit or jacket already, extend its usefulness by adding blouses or shells in each of your five colors:

essence, romantic, dramatic, energy, and *tranquil.* Bingo! Now you have five different outfits, especially if you highlight each color's unique effects by adding jewelry, a scarf, or other accessories that focus on that special energy.

What to Buy

If you can buy only one new outfit, get a suit or a suitlike jacket in your **First Base** unless you have a very casual lifestyle, in which case, choose the **Base** that matches your needs. Then gradually add blouses or shells in each of your five colors: *essence, romantic, dramatic, energy,* and *tranquil,* and pick up accessories as needed. The first three colors on that list will dress your outfit up, especially if you add some metallic jewelry. The last two colors on that list will make your outfit more casual, especially if you add some matte jewelry. The different energies of these five colors will make it look as though your one suit is five completely different outfits.

MY AUTHENTIC STYLE SHOPPING LIST:

MY SUIT OR JACKET IN FIRST, SECOND, OR THIRD BASE:
My blouse or shell in *essence* **color:** _____
My blouse or shell in *romantic* **color:** _____
My blouse or shell in *dramatic* **color:** _____

My blouse or shell in *energy* color: _____

My blouse or shell in *tranquil* color: _____

DRESSES

Fixing a So-so Garment

If you have a multicolored dress that is almost right—say, one or two of three colors are correct—then find some jewelry or other accessories that will bring out the right colors. If you have a solid dress that is almost right—say, it's a greenish brown rather than the warmer reddish brown that is right for you— then find some jewelry or other accessories that will bring out the right tone.

For example, suppose you're a Tawny Spring and you have a dress with a pattern that mixes coral, black, and white. The black and white aren't really your **true colors,** but the coral is. Jewelry or a scarf that focuses on the coral would help focus the eye on the tones you like, making the black and white less important.

Or suppose you're a Bronze Autumn and your red-brown dress isn't quite the shade of chocolate that you now know is one of your **true colors.** Perhaps a jade necklace or a bronze pin will cue the eye in the right direction, until you can afford to purchase a garment that is perfect in every way.

You can also add a jacket or a cardigan to your dress, perhaps with a scarf or some jewelry that pulls the two garments together. This can serve two purposes: It corrects a not-quite-right dress and it extends the usefulness of your A-plus dress, which looks like one outfit without the jacket and like a completely other outfit with it.

However, don't go out and buy new garments to correct your almost rights! From now on, any major purchase that you make should be a genuine A-plus, not something intended to correct a B-minus.

Making Every Garment Go Further

Dresses aren't generally as good as suits for varying your effect, but they are good for an instant head-to-toe look that doesn't necessarily need many accessories. With the right dress, you may not need a jacket, a belt, a necklace, or anything else—just put the dress on and you're done!

If you do want to make one dress look like several, however, here are some suggestions. Not all of these options will work for every dress, but experiment a little and see what effects you can achieve.

- Wear your A-plus dress with a *jacket* or *cardigan* in a matching or contrasting color.
- Wear it with a cute *belt* in a matching or contrasting color.
- Add *metallic jewelry* or a *sparkly pashmina* for an evening look.
- Add *matte jewelry* for a daytime look.
- Put on some *strappy sandals* for evening fun.
- Try *tall boots* for a more casual air.

What to Buy

MY AUTHENTIC STYLE SHOPPING LIST:

ACCESSORIES FOR A VERSATILE DRESS:	
1.	_____
2.	_____
3.	_____
4.	_____

SLACKS AND SKIRTS

Fixing a So-so Garment

Here you're in luck because slacks and skirts are farthest away from your face. If they're almost right, they're the last item you need to replace. Over time, I want you to have only A-plus garments in your closet, and so eventually, you will brighten your wardrobe by purchasing some perfect pants and skirts as the almost rights wear out. Meanwhile, though, concentrate on getting the upper garments to look good and worry less about the lower ones.

Making Every Garment Go Further

As with your suits and jackets, you can extend the look of your slacks and skirts by varying the blouse, shell, or sweater that goes with them. You have a few different choices:

1. Add shells in five of your *true colors—essence, romantic, dramatic, energy,* and *tranquil*—and pick up accessories as needed. As we've seen, the first three colors on that list will dress your outfit up, perhaps with some metallic jewelry or a metallic scarf of bronze, silver, or gold. The last two colors on that list will make your outfit more casual, especially if you add some wooden jewelry, some handmade beads, or a woven scarf.

2. Choose shells in colors that match your pants and skirts and then add jewelry, a scarf, a jacket, or a wrap in a contrasting color. A *First Base* pants-and-shell outfit, for example, under a *romantic* jacket is an instant wow. A *Second Base* pants-and-sweater outfit with a *tranquil* scarf and some *energy*-colored jewelry will make a warm and relaxed outfit that brings out your best energies. A *Third Base* capri-and-tank outfit with a *dramatic* pair of dangly earrings can add some sizzle to your beach-party outfit. You get the idea: mix, match, and experiment!

Shirts, Blouses, and Other Tops

Fixing a So-so Garment

These garments are the easiest to replace, of course, because they tend to be the least expensive. However, you still may need to make do with several almost-rights before you find the time and/or money to replace them. Here are some suggestions for correcting your almost-right tops:

1. If you're wearing the almost-right top with a correct neutral, choose accessories and jewelry that bring out the neutral. If you're wearing the almost-right top with an almost-right neutral, choose accessories and jewelry that correct the neutral.
2. If you're wearing the almost-right top with a correct color, choose accessories and jewelry that bring out that correct color.
3. If you're wearing the almost-right top with an almost-right color, choose accessories and jewelry of a correct neutral color, such as a mahogany wood bracelet to correct an aubergine top, or a dove-gray metallic scarf to correct a slate blouse.

In all of these cases, you're looking for a scarf or piece of jewelry that has your own ***true colors*** in it but that tries to correct or harmonize with your almost-right outfit, *not* to contrast with it. Contrast (of varying degrees, depending on your ***Archetype***) is terrific if all your colors are correct. But if you're not starting with your ***true colors,*** contrast just adds disharmony to an already "noisy" situation.

Making Every Garment Go Further

We've already seen how to use tops to extend suits, jackets, slacks, and skirts, and how accessories can vary your look even more. You might set aside a couple of hours in which you try on every possible combination of your garments and accessories, just so you have the mental energy to create some new combinations when you're not pressed for time.

What to Buy

MY AUTHENTIC STYLE SHOPPING LIST:

TOPS IN SOME OF MY TRUE COLORS
1. _____
2. _____
3. _____
4. _____

ACCESSORIES IN MY AUTHENTIC STYLE
1. _____
2. _____

Accessories in My Authentic Style	
3.	_____
4.	_____

Summer, Autumn, and Spring Coats

You may be able to fix an almost-right coat with the right scarf. Here's a more unusual idea: Try replacing the buttons in a correct version of the coat's color or neutral. The correct buttons can help cue the eye away from the incorrect color.

What to Buy

Buttons:	
1.	_____
Accessories:	
1.	_____
2.	_____
3.	_____

Winter and Formal Coats

The previous coat suggestions will work here, too, but you have a few extra options: gloves, a hat, even a shawl or pashmina that wraps around or drapes over the coat. It may be hard finding coats in your true colors, but luckily, accessories can often go a long way toward correcting the problem!

What to Buy

Buttons:	
1.	_____
Accessories:	
1.	_____
2.	_____
3.	_____

A Coat for All Seasons

If you're trying to figure out what to wear *outside* your fabulous new outfits, here are some suggestions. Remember that you can always use hats, scarves, gloves, and other accessories in your **true colors** to vary the look of any coat.

Formal Coat—*First Base*

Winter Coat—Depending on how formal you want to go, *First Base, Second Base,* or *Third Base*

> I encourage a second, "fun" coat in your *romantic* or *dramatic* color.
>
> Summer Coat—*Third Base*
>
> Autumn Raincoat—*Essence Color*
>
> Spring Raincoat—A lighter, pastel version of your *romantic, dramatic, energy,* or *tranquil* color

Prepare Your Shopping List

Now that you've analyzed your wardrobe, you can begin to make a shopping list. For suggestions on how to work the aisles of your favorite store, see the next chapter.

Creating Your Authentic Style: Look at the notes you've made in this chapter, and decide which items are most important to you. Then make a shopping list, listing your purchases in order of priority. As time and budget allow, add those garments to your wardrobe, using the shopping techniques described in the next chapter. Here is one possible suggestion for how to organize your list:

OUTFITS THAT ALMOST WORK

	OUTFIT	ACCESSORIES NEEDED TO MAKE IT WORK
1.	_____	_____
2.	_____	_____

	OUTFIT	ACCESSORIES NEEDED TO MAKE IT WORK
3.	_____	_____
4.	_____	_____
5.	_____	_____

MY *AUTHENTIC STYLE* SHOPPING LIST:

My suit or jacket in *First, Second,* or *Third Base:* _____

My blouse or shell in *essence* color: _____

My blouse or shell in *romantic* color: _____

My blouse or shell in *dramatic* color: _____

My blouse or shell in *energy* color: _____

My blouse or shell in *tranquil* color: _____

Accessories to fix Outfit #1: _____

Accessories to fix Outfit #2: _____

Accessories to fix Outfit #3: _____

Accessories to fix Outfit #4: _____	

Accessories to fix Outfit #5: _____	

My dress in one of my true colors: _____	

ACCESSORIES FOR MY DRESS	
1.	_____
2.	_____
3.	_____

MY SLACKS OR SKIRTS IN ONE OF MY TRUE COLORS	
1.	_____
2.	_____
3.	_____

ACCESSORIES OR BUTTONS TO FIX MY COATS	
1.	_____
2.	_____
3.	_____

10

seeing the world
through lime-colored glasses:

shopping for your authentic style

some of us love shopping and are really good at it. We sail through the store, zeroing in on one fabulous garment after another, emerging with a treasure trove of satisfying purchases.

But for many of us, shopping is an ordeal, a grueling experiment in frustration as we struggle to find even one outfit that we think of as flattering. Every purchase seems to take forever, and at the end of the day, we're pretty sure that we'll have to return most garments anyway, or settle for second best.

If you're in that second group, don't despair. Yes, shopping is a skill—but it's a skill you can learn. And in this chapter, I'm going to teach you how to do it.

SHOPPING SERENITY: A STEP-BY-STEP APPROACH

Rome wasn't built in a day—and your wardrobe won't be, either! Here's a step-by-step approach to finding the purchases that are on your shopping list:

Step One:
Give Yourself Enough Time

As we'll soon see, you'll eventually be able to nip into a store between a visit to the dentist and a trip to Mommy and Me class with the kids. But if you're not used to shopping efficiently, allow yourself at least three hours of total "me" time for your first attempt at shopping for your ***authentic style***. Ideally you'll choose a day when your schedule is truly open-ended, but at the very least, allow yourself an entire morning or afternoon. Go by yourself or with a friend you trust, and prepare to concentrate on yourself.

Friends: To Bring or Not to Bring?

Okay, here's the problem with nine out of ten friends that you might bring with you on your first Shopping for ***Authentic Style*** trip: They won't know what looks good on you. They simply won't. They're likely to know what's good on *them*. But unless they're quite unusual—and I think that nine out of ten figure is fairly accurate—they'll confuse clothes that work for them with garments that flatter you. They steer you wrong out of love, perhaps. But they will often steer you wrong.

If you are sure your friend can look at your color choices and will respect your need to follow this system, then by all means, bring her along. Sometimes two heads *are* better than one. But if you feel the least little bit of doubt about your friend's objectivity, meet her for lunch tomorrow and preserve your shopping privacy today.

Step Two:
Look Your Best

Your goal for this trip is to solidify your idea of an A-plus look. (You might not even buy anything if you can't find items that make the grade.) If you've just discovered which colors, clothes, and objects express your true self, you're probably not used to looking your absolute best every single time you leave the house. Give yourself a boost by shopping in an outfit that's as close to perfect as you can make it. Choose garments from your newly organized closet that fit, flatter, and boost your spirits. Then, every time you try on something new, you can start by looking at the A-plus version of you first. That's your baseline. Does the new item measure up?

Naturally you should give yourself all the help you can in seeing yourself as objectively as possible. If you'd normally wear makeup with the outfit you're going to buy—a power suit or a dressy dress—wear the same makeup on this shopping trip. Make sure your haircut hasn't expired. If you usually avoid glasses in favor of your contacts, put in your contacts. And either wear or bring along the shoes and hose that you expect to pair with your new purchase.

You should also make sure that your undergarments fit perfectly. Check out my Web site for some help in finding a place that can fit you if you're not sure about your bra. If you don't have undergarments that you're happy with, make them your first purchase. Even if nobody but you ever sees them, it's important that they work well.

Step Three:
This First Time Out, Choose a Large Store

I love small businesses and I would normally urge you to support them. But for this first trip, you probably want a bit more anonymity than is easy to get in a tiny boutique. A large department store will usually offer you more privacy—and a wider selection of clothes.

If a saleswoman approaches with a polite "May I help you?" make sure you're equally polite. Ask for her name and assure her that you'll come find her when it's time to make your purchases, so she knows she'll get her credit. If you're ready to try something on, ask for her help in setting up a dressing room. Don't, however, feel obligated to let her help you. First of all, you want the practice in identifying and choosing your own garments to try on. Second, you don't want to bond with her and then feel guilty if you don't like any of her choices. One quick look at Oscar night should convince you that even top stylists don't always dress their clients well. Why let a possibly uninformed opinion interfere with your own process of looking and choosing?

Step Four:
Start with Your True *Colors*

You have two choices here. If you can handle a multitude of choices, just look around the department you're in and put on those lime-colored glasses; that is, start seeing the world through the prism of your palette. Zero in on any hue that you know is one of your true colors, and look only at garments in those colors.

Or, if that sounds overwhelming—and at first it often is—just focus on *one* of your **true colors.** If you're looking for a **First Base** power suit, go to the departments where suits are sold and focus your mind's eye on your **First Base.** If you've used paint chips to identify your colors, bring along your **First Base** chip. Or perhaps you already own another garment in the color you want; if so, bring it along. However you can, support yourself in identifying the correct version of your color.

With your color or colors firmly in your mind, walk through the store, department by department, scanning for the shade(s) you want. If a department is full of black, white, and red items and your **true colors** are sea-foam, powder pink, and dove gray, you can skip the whole department, saving yourself at least half an hour to spend somewhere that's far more likely to offer you a better selection. Perhaps a department will offer you only one or two choices, or perhaps you'll find ten or twelve. Either way, put on those lime-colored glasses and look *only* for lime-colored garments—or whatever color(s) you've decided are right for you.

Step Five:
Consider Price, Care, and Usefulness to You

Can you afford this garment? Does it require hand washing or dry cleaning that you're unwilling to do or unable to afford? Does it look as though it will fall apart after one trip to the laundromat? Is it something you even need, let alone something on the shopping list you started to write in the previous chapter?

Now, when you're first learning to recognize your **true colors** and your **authentic style,** you may want to try on a garment even if the answer to all these questions would otherwise lead you to leave it on the rack. I want you to see yourself wearing as many suitable garments as possible, so you can expand and solidify your A-plus vision of yourself, gradually coming to accept nothing less.

So this first time out, you might put aside an otherwise perfect garment that you don't really intend to buy. And who knows? When you see how terrific you look in it, maybe you'll decide to expand your dry-cleaning budget!

Lose the Label!

No matter which designer takes credit for your garment, try to ignore the label and just focus on how the garment makes you look. If you love a designer but can't wear his or her latest line, so be it. Till you start getting paid to wear the wrong clothes, don't wear them!

Likewise, ignore the labels that tell you the size. Don't say to yourself, "I just can't bear to own a size fourteen," or "This seems to fit but I know the size is wrong." Some designers cut small, some big, and every one is different. Sizes also vary depending on which part of the world your garment comes from.

So ignore the label—you can even ignore the garment. Focus instead on how *you* look in the garment. In the end, that's all that really matters.

Step Six:
Try on the Garments You've Selected

We talked in the previous chapter about how to try on garments. An A-plus garment will make you smile with delight when you first see yourself in it, so if that reaction is missing or too slow in coming, be wary. Be aware that a garment in one of your true colors may still not have the right shape; or the shape may be perfect while the fit is wrong. Make sure you can move easily in the garment you've chosen, with your own natural stride and posture. If you find yourself shortening your step or slouching in an unnatural curve, you're probably wearing the wrong choice.

You should also make sure to try on every single garment you're considering. Many clothing lines are made overseas now, often in many different countries. That blue blazer may be identical to the black one in the same style—but the blue may be cut small while the black is cut big. I've had clients tell me that a tank in one color flattered their bust line, while the same size tank in the same style but a different color gapped or bunched or cut their armpits at the wrong angle. Even two versions of the same black blazer—say, the one you initially tried on, with the torn lining, and the replacement garment from the back that the saleswoman pulled for you—may fit differently. Try *everything*.

Step Seven:
Allow Yourself Not to Buy Anything

Yes, it would be nice if you started filling up your closet right away, but I'm far more concerned that you continue the process of learning how to see. Besides, since you've just emptied your closet, you don't want to refill it with the wrong garments. I hope you find lots of nice purchases on your first or second shopping trips, but I'd rather you said no to all the wrong garments and held out for something better.

Admirable Alterations

Although I don't want you buying a single garment that isn't perfect, it doesn't need to be perfect right away. Sometimes a garment can be made perfect through alterations.

Let's say you find the perfect suit jacket but the skirt that goes with it is just a bit too wide. You may find it more economical to pay to have the skirt taken in a bit rather than letting this great suit go. Often department and specialty stores will do the alterations for you, for a relatively small price. Otherwise you might have to find a local tailor—perhaps working out of your dry-cleaning store—to help you with this.

KEEPING YOUR EYE ON THE ESSENTIALS

When I was fresh out of design school, I would often find myself designing the costumes for Off-Off Broadway shows that had tiny budgets—like, fifty dollars to costume a dozen people in the garments of nineteenth-century Russia. "Anything that's left over, you can keep," the twenty-two-year-old producers would tell me grandly, and of course, I'd end up supplementing my costume budget out of my own minuscule bank account.

What I learned from these challenging shows, however, was to focus on the essentials. Obviously I didn't have the money to buy or rent elaborate costumes for everyone in the cast—or even for *anyone* in the cast! I had to ask myself, "What is the one item that will bring this character to life?" and then go for that.

If you're shopping on a budget—and these days, who isn't?—you'll want to do the same thing. Use the shopping list in the previous chapter to help you develop your own list of must-haves. Then, when you go shopping, scan for those. Follow the step-by-step process I've suggested: Try on only those few things that make the grade on the store floor, and be very picky about what you purchase. "A-plus or nothing" should become your new motto, even as you're zeroing in on the priority garments that you need next.

SHOPPING FOR CHRISTMAS IN THE MIDDLE OF JULY

After your closet is 80 percent full, then you get to switch to another type of shopping. Now your goal is no longer to fill up your closet with your essential garments, but rather to plug the few little gaps that still remain. Great news: You're now ready for "lifelong shopping!"

Ideally, once your closet is mainly full, you'll learn how to keep an eye out for the items that will enhance your wardrobe, so that you're continually replenishing and updating your outfits without becoming overwhelmed by the need to shop. Whether shopping is your favorite retail therapy, a detested chore, or something in between, you'll find ideas in this chapter that make your relationship to shopping—and your wardrobe—easier and more relaxed.

KEEPING AN EYE OUT FOR "YOUR" CLOTHES

If you're out and about, and you come across a garment that seems right for you, I highly encourage you to snap it up if you can do so without economic hardship, especially if it's an unusual color, fabric, cut, or style. You never know when you're going to see a garment like that again, so seize the moment and buy something that you know will look great on you and that you'll eventually wear often, even if you don't need it right now.

Likewise, if you see items on sale that you know are going to be right for you, take advantage of the lower prices while you can. Poke your head into boutiques, visit designer sample sales, even stop by some outlet stores.

Of course, on your initial forays into shopping for your **authentic style,** you may find it overwhelming to shop this way. It's important that you focus your first excursions onto the basic wardrobe items you need immediately, and that you stay very clear about the colors, clothes, and accessories that work for you.

Later in the process, though, your selection of A-plus garments will come to seem almost automatic. That's when you can expose yourself to an otherwise dizzying array of choices. Your trained eye will filter out 99 percent of the clothing that surrounds you, allowing you to notice only the three items in the store that you could ever possibly wear. Perhaps a closer look will reveal that two out of those three outfits aren't right for you after all. That leaves you just one garment to try on—and a high level of confidence about deciding on the spot whether it's A-plus or below-grade.

Shopping at a Distance: Catalogue and Online Shopping

As you might imagine, I'm very particular about fit, and I want to make sure you buy only garments that fit you perfectly. Likewise, a slightly different shade might be enough to make the difference between "true color" and "not right for you." Both of these factors can make it extremely difficult to shop from paper or online catalogues.

Still, there are some terrific bargains in catalogues, and no one can argue with convenience. So here are some suggestions that can improve your "remote shopping" results:

- ***When in doubt, pull out the measuring tape.*** Every online or paper catalogue includes a size chart with measurements. If you're not sure what size you are in this company's terms, measure yourself and find out. As always, ignore the emotional attachments to the size you think you "should" be and just focus on getting a correct fit.

- ***Look at both the catalogue descriptions and as many pictures as you can find.*** If an online catalogue offers multiple views, take them up on their offer. Try to imagine yourself wearing the garment and remember that you probably don't have the model's coloring or figure. Your purchase should not be based on what *she* looks good in, but on what *you* look good in!

- ***Go by the sight of each color, not by its label.*** Often the color given by the catalogue won't match your idea of a color. Maybe the catalogue will say, "wheat," and you think, "off white." Or perhaps it says, "evergreen," and you think, "deep jade." Don't worry—just go by what you see.

- ***Leave yourself an "out."*** Your commitment is to owning only A-plus garments, and until you've tried on a piece of clothing, you often can't be sure how well it's going to work. Color, size, fit, and style can all look different in a picture than they do in real life. So unless you're 100 percent certain that you want something, avoid final sales and no-return sales in catalogues, and make sure you're willing to spend the time and effort to ship something back to the company if it doesn't work as well as it could. Generally you'll want to avoid express shipping, since delivery costs are usually not refunded when you return an item.

Your Guide to Lifelong Shopping

Here are the principles that can help guide you through your lifelong shopping experience:

1. *If something works, keep going back to that well.* Some stores seem to offer a wide variety of items that are right for you—keep returning for their sales and even their regular days and see if anything new has come in that might work.

2. *If the "well" changes, be ready to change, too.* Again, you're not buying the label. If a chain store or one-of-a-kind boutique used to have great clothes for you and now doesn't seem to, accept the loss and move on.

3. *Stick with the styles and colors that you know will work, even as you continue to branch out.* If you understand which colors, clothes, and objects express your authentic self, you'll probably develop a kind of uniform that always works for you: a blazer and turtleneck, for example, or a cardigan and slacks. I want you to be adventurous—but I also want you to learn which outfits you can always rely on. Then on your lifelong shopping journey you can look out for both the tried-and-true and the super-brand-new.

4. *Become bolder over time.* Are there colors or types of clothes that you've wondered about but haven't yet incorporated into your wardrobe? Have I suggested some wardrobe ideas that you've so far avoided? After your basic wardrobe is hanging safely in your closet, consider experimenting with some of the

more far-out touches. Your whole look may "pop" more as a result.

5. ***Stay true to your own opinions.*** I'm sure, if you're seeking out your **true colors** and embracing your **authentic style,** that your look is becoming more "you." Most of the people in your life will support you on your journey—but some will not. You'll encounter some jealous people who can't stand to see you looking so good, and some well-meaning people who can only see your wardrobe in terms of what might look good on *them.* Learn to filter out these unhelpful opinions and trust your own eye.

6. ***Continue to let things go.*** Maybe now you'll have the courage to release some of the pieces you couldn't let go of when you were first cleaning out your closet. Everybody makes mistakes. If you've bought something and not worn it for a year, or if you know well before then that this new garment doesn't work, get it out of your closet to make room for something else.

7. ***Start your own "style file."*** We costume designers rarely begin a project without doing research: collecting images from books, magazines, newspapers, and postcards that evoke the feeling of a character, period, or setting. Now it's time for you to do your own research. Start keeping a file of images that you feel express a part of your personality or appearance. If you respond strongly to a painting, a dress in a catalogue, a postcard, or a photograph, toss it into your style file so you can start refreshing your eyes and your spirit with these images that resonate with

you. They'll help you find clothing that speaks to you, too.

THE BEAUTY OF HAVING A SYSTEM

A few years ago, I did a consultation with an actress in Toronto who later managed to drag in her husband, kicking and screaming, for his own session with me. This was a woman who for years had been unable to interest her husband in shopping with her. Maybe once a year she'd manage to persuade him to come into a store while she tried things on and he'd sit glowering with a book and wait for her to be done.

I did the man's palette and had a long talk with him about first-time shopping and lifelong shopping. Imagine my surprise when my actress client called me the day after our meeting.

"You'll never guess where my husband is," she told me breathlessly. "He's at the mall! He's actually gone shopping *by himself*!"

Later, when I spoke with the man, it all made sense. For years, he'd never known how to think about shopping. Feeling overwhelmed, he simply avoided it. Now that he had such a clear idea of what looked good on him and some idea of how to filter out what didn't, he was able to handle the often upsetting experience of visiting a mall stuffed to the gills with too many choices. No longer overwhelmed by the process, he was able to focus—and choose well.

So enjoy your lifelong shopping! It's definitely the time when you profit from all your hard work—and in the best of circumstances, your closet will profit, too!

conclusion:

the colors of your life

NOW that you understand your *true colors* and your *authentic style,* you're well on the way to re-creating your closet and transforming your wardrobe. You're fully committed to ensuring that every garment makes you look and feel great because it is an authentic visual manifestation of who you are. Congratulations! Here are some final suggestions for creating your own unique *authentic style:*

KEEP EXPLORING AND UPDATING YOUR STYLE

Like most other important tasks, developing a unique style takes ongoing work. Just as you need to visit the dentist for regular checkups, you need to regularly check in with yourself to maintain your authentic style.

You may have noticed people who don't update their styles to reflect who they have now become. Think of that forty-five-year-old neighbor who's still sporting the same hairdo that she had in high school, say, long hair falling to her waist with the occasionally trimmed bangs. Perhaps your neighbor knew that she looked adorable at age sixteen in that hairstyle— but now? In her mind it looks just as good as it did then. You might be wondering, "Why does Sylvie have her hair like that?" There may be many reasons, but chances are that years ago, she got a lot of attention looking that way and she is afraid of changing the formula, even though that formula now functions against her.

As you continue to honor your *authentic style,* I'd like you to think about the elements you want to hold on to and the elements you might like to change. I'm not suggesting change for change's sake. But I do strongly believe that after embracing your *true colors* and your *authentic style,* you will find new ways to become more and more yourself. You'll be changing your style both to make it more expressive of who you are, and to keep up with the ways that "who you are" is changing.

To this end, I recommend seasonal Style Checkups of your style, closet, and makeup. I have found that many of my clients shop for their *true colors* but start out playing it a bit safe when it comes to their accessories and the more theatrical elements of their *authentic style.* Are you really wearing the brightest version of your *romantic* color? Have you always yearned to be a "lady who wears hats" but have never quite dared to play with that particular accessory? Once you've mastered the basic principles of your *authentic style,* you might consider taking it a bit further as you conduct four Style Checkups each year.

Your Quarterly Style Checkup

1. *Check your closet.* Have you kept the order to your closet and honored it as your space? If not, con-

sider the ways that poor closet maintenance makes it harder for you to keep up your look. Imagine what would happen if you went shoe shopping at your favorite department store and found ladies' shoes mixed in with house wares and pet supplies. Wouldn't you be confused and frustrated by how jarring the environment was, and wouldn't that make it harder to focus on your look and to have a successful shopping excursion? Getting dressed at the doors of your sacred "Shrine Sarita" or "Altar of Alice" will be equally jarring if you don't maintain a well-organized and inviting space.

2. *Check your almost-rights.* What about those not-quite-right clothes that you pushed to the right side of your closet? Have you worn any of them? I'm guessing no. If these near misses have not made it to the far left side by the time of your first Quarterly Checkup, let's face it: They never will. Call that resale shop for another pickup and brighten someone else's life with your discards.

3. *Check your lifestyle.* Have you changed jobs recently? Did you go from Domestic Goddess to Executive Powerhouse? You can't change your type, but you can always change your lifestyle. You won't be able to relax and enjoy your stay-at-home-mom days if all your clothes are office oriented; you won't be as successful in the corporate world if you're dressing like a soccer mom. Make sure your clothes reflect the way you're living your life.

4. *Check your changes.* Maybe in the last three months you've had a major life change, in circumstance, outlook, or perhaps both. Have you married?

Divorced? Started dating? Fallen in love? Did you get promoted at work? Switch careers? Start to free-lance? Seen your youngest off to college? Maybe you've hit a bump in the road, either at work or in your personal life. Or perhaps you're going through a period of questioning and reflection as you reconsider decisions you made a long time ago.

Believe it or not, times of intense change are actually the perfect time to revisit your *authentic style.* I know it can be difficult sometimes to keep expressing yourself as you are going through changes, but your new incarnation offers you new opportunities to draw on the personal power and spiritual support that both your *true colors* and your *authentic style* can offer you. Times of great change, while often challenging, can be the perfect time to become *more* of who you are. So ask yourself, "Does my closet telegraph who I am right now?"

5. *Check your wardrobe.* Look at the clothes hanging in your closet and ask yourself what they say about you. If they were the wardrobe of a character in a novel or a movie, what five words would you use to describe that character? Take a moment to jot them down in a journal or notebook, along with today's date. Three months from now you can come up with new ones if you like, but meanwhile, these five words should be thought of as your personal dry cleaning—your way of keeping your look fresh!

Create Your Own Unique *Authentic Style*

Once you've fully embraced your **Archetype,** you are ready for the next step: creating your own unique **authentic style.** You begin to put together your own unique way of dressing and accessorizing and presenting yourself that can't be mistaken for anyone else in the world's. Your style becomes so individual that friends, relatives, and even colleagues start to associate you with particular pieces of clothing or jewelry. They'll see a skirt or a necklace or a bag and say, "Oh, that looks like something Lisa might wear," or "Nikki would look good in that, wouldn't she?"

The wonderful thing about developing your own style is that it shows more than what looks good on you, more than what flatters your coloring or figure—flattering though your wardrobe will certainly be. Your **authentic style** reveals the real *you*: your feisty spirit, or your gentle humor, or your sensuous and adventurous side. It takes a certain amount of courage to reveal yourself to that extent, and more than a little self-knowledge. But that's what is so exciting about this ultimate expression of your **authentic style**: the way it expresses your true self while challenging you to become the truest version of yourself that you can possibly be.

Starting the Day Out Right: Full-Body Smiling

A smile is the building block of good posture and the key to a more free, relaxed self. Contrary to popular opinion, smiling does not cease with the ends of your mouth, nor with the plane of your face. Observe toddlers whose feet can barely stay on the ground as they float with happiness, their voices reaching notes higher than any known scale. Like them, you should allow

yourself to smile throughout your entire body. This is a terrific
way to get ready to present yourself to the world. Try it while
standing in front of a mirror in natural bright lighting:

1. ***Recall a happy time.*** With your feet slightly spread
    apart and your eyes closed, breathe naturally and
    think of the person, place, thing, or experience that
    immediately makes you happy. You're going for
    that wonderful feeling of pure, simple happiness,
    uncomplicated by any stress or thoughts of doubt.
    Take as much time as you need to feel the light of
    happiness fill up every part of your body, letting go of
    any tension that might taint your joy in any way.

2. ***Become aware of your body.*** Notice that as your
    happiness grows, your shoulders relax, your lower
    back releases, and your ankles cease to lock, freeing
    you from the need to shift your feet.

3. ***Open your eyes.*** Look into the mirror and observe
    what a real smile looks like. Let it linger as you feel
    throughout your body the tingling effects of full-
    body smiling.

4. ***Appreciate yourself.*** As you continue to smile, observe
    your whole self in the mirror. Appreciate something
    physical about yourself—the first thing that hits
    you—perhaps the beautiful green-gold flecks in your
    eyes, the geometrically arched shape of your brow, the
    olive glow of your cheek, or your delicate, sensitive
    hands.

5. ***Carry the feeling forward.*** Convince yourself that
    the next person that you come in contact with is
    noticing that exact thing about you—and watch your
    confidence grow. This is the confidence you want

to take with you when you go on to choose new clothes and discard some old ones. Every outfit you put on should make you feel as good as you do right now!

Remember: Just as everyone has her own unique *authentic style,* so does everyone have her own unique authentic smile! Some people's true smiles are huge and vibrant while others' are relaxed and subtle. Let your smile be your own.

EMBRACING THE COLOR OF YOUR STYLE

Ultimately, your true colors and your authentic style aren't limited to your clothes: They can extend to your possessions, your home, your workplace—any object you own and any space you inhabit. As you come to embrace your authentic style, you'll begin to think of ways that you can express your unique qualities throughout your life, and you'll see how doing so can be an empowering and joyous experience. True colors and authentic style aren't just about fashion and clothes and beauty, they're about discovering and expressing who you truly are.

Maybe you're a therapist who's chosen one of your *true colors* for your stationery or your business card to express your nurturing personality or your ability to look calmly at a problem and tell the truth about it. Perhaps you're an executive whose office colors, furniture, and ornaments proclaim, "I'm energetic, enthusiastic, and good at getting the job done." Maybe you're a parent whose kids' friends always want to come over because the colors and style of your playroom say, "Everyone is welcome to have fun here," or perhaps you're a hard-working accountant whose vacation home instantly surrounds you with a soothing, relaxing aura that helps you to recover when you retreat there after April fifteenth.

Whatever your intentions, your *true colors* and your *authentic style* can help make you more comfortable in all areas of your world. They can help you know yourself better—and then they can enable you to show the world who you really are. I've seen it time and time again: When a woman embraces her *true colors* and her *authentic style,* she claims her own beauty, her own power, and her own capacity to love. And when she's done all that, life's riches surely follow.

By reading this book, you've begun an amazing journey. I wish you luck along the way.

> For a list of places to shop and resources I recommend to help you get started finding your true colors, please visit my Web site: www.davidzyla.com.

acknowledgments

t<small>O</small> my parents, Raymond and Carole, who were my first clients . . .
When I was five.

My most sincere thanks and professional respect to these talented artisans who contributed so much to this book: Amy Hertz, Celeste Fine, Rachel Kranz, Christine Ball, Liza Cassity, Melissa Miller, Grace McQuade, Lynn Goldberg, Monica Benalcazar, Spring Hoteling, and Liz Stein.

I'd like to extend a very special thank-you to these individuals who somehow found the time in their busy schedules to read at least one draft of *The Color of Style*—you helped the process profoundly: Michele Bowbyes, Carla Dunham, Lili Forouraghi, Julie Galdieri, Frances Poe, Patricia O'Connell, MaryKatherine Ryan, Grace Sette, Linda Zagaria, and Carole Zyla.

I'm proud to be a part of the art, design, fashion, entertainment, and media communities, and specifically thank these members who've supported me with this project: Evangeline Benedetti, Phillip Bloch, Carla Dunham, Jonathan Fong, Shawn Ray Fons, Jay Godfrey, Robin Hommel, Brooke Johnson, John Jones, Susan Lucci, Michael Macko, Mary Norton, Aaron Shure, Jo-ey Tang, Carmen Marc Valvo, and Heidi Weisel.

The process of writing this book reminded me how fortunate I am that my life is abundant with such talented and connected individuals.

9 *acknowledgments*

I am extremely grateful to: Jason Arbuckle, Anna Balkan, Kevin Berg, Marika Brancato, Richard Butterfield, Stephen Cali, Joyce Chang, Enza Dolce, Tom Handley, Erin Harrington, Jonathan Herzog, Carla Iliescu, Vicky Ioannou, Debbie Karch, Anthony Pascarelli, Brian Ragan, Hope Schultz, Jeff Weiner, and Gabby Winkel.

Additionally, I send my gratitude to my clients, colleagues, and friends who have served as my inspiration for this book and my continued belief in the transformative power of color: Mark Arena, Margot Astrachan, Dee Baker, Michelle Baker, Esther Blum, Christopher Boshears, Suzanne Caygill, Bill Connington, Kevin Duda, Abby Harper, Gail Harper, Vy Higginsen, Chad Larabee, Eleanor Leinen, Moira Quirk, Michael Raynor, Becky Rohr, Marianna Rosett, Tracey Segal, Ruth Shure, Vicki Tashjian, Peter Williams, and Ross Znavor.

And lastly, I toast Chris Poe for his encouragement, advice, and limitless support of *The Color of Style*.